Larry Ukali
Johnson-Redd

Long Distance Love
(This is a memoir of my second trip to Nigeria and my engagement to a Nigerian Woman)

The Reading Glass
BOOKS

The Reading Glass Books
(888) 420-3050
www.readingglassbooks.com
fulfillment@readingglassbooks.com

Long Distance Love

By: Larry Ukali Johnson-Redd

Acknowledgement

Link:

http://www.amazon.com/Long-Distance-Love-ebook/dp/B003XRE66G/ ref=sr_1_3? s=books&ie=UTF8&qid=1280735927&sr=1-3

Long Distance Love is very personal memoir of my 2005 Trip to Nigeria, West Africa. The International Standard Book Number for this great and international travel/ Romance/ Memoir Book LONG DISTANCE LOVE is 0-9785772-7-2.

Dedication

This book Long Distance Love is dedicated to all of those people in the world who are looking for the real love and have not yet found it. Thus book is a sequel in many ways to Journey To The Motherland, From San Francisco To Benin City (2002) that is available currently at my Amazon.com page. So this book is also dedicated to African-Americans and other readers interested in learning more about Africa, as well as Nigeria in particular. This book is also dedicated to Nigerians and other Africans who want to learn more about African-Americans and America.

Many thanks to Rudolph Lewis for my table at the Chicken bones Online Magazine and the interview that appears in this book.

I will publish a completely audio version of Loving Black Women by September 1, 2010. And the 2 CD Set titled LOVING BLACK WOMEN—Audio will be available September 2013 through my Journey Books page on Amazon.com at this link:
http://www.amazon.com/gp/offer-listing/0967422663/ref=dp_olp_1?ie=UTF8&qid=1279781516&sr=1-1-fkmr0

Chicken Bones On-Line Magazine Link:
http://www.nathanielturner.com/

Journal Of Pan African Studies Link:
http://www.jpanafrican.com/

Please Read My Other Books

I hope you will read this book and respond to me on my facebook page using my name on facebook to locate my page. I also hope you will visit me on You Tube and read my other books. I am publishing Long Distance Love for the first time a kindle Book at the same time I am publishing this book American Challenges In The Obama Era. I am also publishing **Long Distance Love. Long Distance Love** is a memoir of my 2005 trip to Nigeria that included a courtship with a young Nigerian woman that some how lasted years later as well as a memorable set of experiences during my 10-day stay in Nigeria, West Africa.

My first book Journey To The Motherland, From San Francisco to Benin City is also available as a paperback book on my Journey Books Page at Amazon.com. for $5.00 plus shipping .The link is:

Journey Books is my book distribution company.

My beloved book History to Destiny, through Afrocentric Poetrycontinues to be out of print however I ask you to give me a donation to help get that book of 304 pages of Spokenword back in print. I have published History To Destiny as a Kindle E Book.. *I have published History To Destiny Through Afrocentric Poetry as an Kindle e-book. Link:*

http://www.amazon.com/gp/offer-listing/0967422663/ref=dp_olp_1?ie=UTF8&qid=1279781516&sr=1-1-fkmr0

Larry Ukali Johnson-Redd—Revised 2010: Biography

Larry Ukali Johnson-Redd, born 1952 in San Francisco, graduated from Balboa High School in 1970 and entered University of San Francisco and received a B.A. in 1974 in Political Science and Ethnic Studies (African American). His quest for education continued at Golden Gate University in San Francisco where he received a Masters in Public Administration 1976 (MPA). In 2004 Ukali earned his Masters of Arts in Educational Administration and his Administrative Credential!

Ukali's books and Black Love Spoken Word:

The Black Expatriate in Africa (1982)

Journey to the Motherland, From San Francisco to Benin City— Autobiographical Novel (2002) Journey To The Motherland from San Francisco to Benin will be published in 2013 as a Kindle e-book.

History To Destiny Through Afrocentric Poetry as a paperback (2004) This is also now an Kindle e-book.

Loving Black Women: Essays and Spoken Word (2006)

New book: 2010—Long Distance Love is now available as a Kindle e-book.

Ukali has delivered his unique Black Love Spoken Word from Sacramento to L. A. to San Francisco to Brooklyn NY! I would love to be invited to your area, program or event as a lecturer, poet or panelist or any combination!

http://www.youtube.com/user/ukalitheafrican

http://www.blackplanet.com/your_page/videos/index.html? profile_id=39945499&profile_name=Ukal2003&user_id=39945499&usernam

http://www.youtube.com/watch?v=uPz7xAnLF9M

http://www.nathanielturner.com/larryuklaijohnsonreddtable.htm

In 2010, Ukali is completing Long Distance Love, by Larry Ukali Johnson-Redd (A Memoir)! Ukali has completed American Challenges in the Obama Era Part 1 in 2010 and is working on Part 2 in 2013

In April 2010 Ukali participated in the SF Kings of Poetry-A DVD will soon be released! Larry can be contacted at 415-425-6711 or **mailto:ljredd52@aol.com**

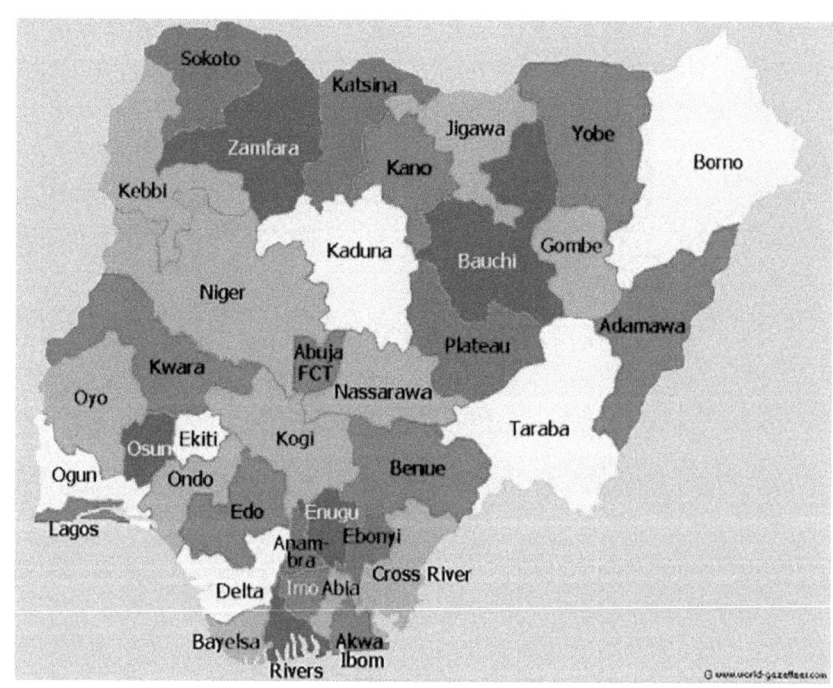

A POLITICAL MAP OF NIGERIA

Check out this link while reading this book and my other books.
http://www.conversationsofafrica.asmnetwork.net/

Preface for Long Distance Love From the author to you

In Africa like everywhere there is good, bad and ugly. More good people of course because most human beings in most countries have something good in them and in Africa, as I remember Nigeria in particular there are a lot of good people! Good people of all religions! Good people who only believe in African Spirits! Good people are the everyday people you see! But there are some bad people everywhere and if you go to Nigeria be sure to read Journey To The Motherland From San Francisco to Benin City and this book to learn about the good, bad and ugly! As you read this book try and decide if this is a real love story or if this is a story about a 419 Queen! I was once told a student 419 person would drive up to the dorm in a brand new car cleaning out some person who sent 5 Thousand Dollars in the false crazy hope that this 419 scheme is going to pay back One Hundred Thousand dollars or more! They will get 1 payment and ask for a second often-smaller payment for transfer fees for the payment! They would then collapse and close every thing down split your money and celebrations begin! Now a days these type letters unfortunately come from all over Africa! These people are doing a lot to shame the image of our motherland and should be stopped immediately because they erode the trust and friendships of Africans all over the world!

First of all what is a 419? I bet you know! But you may not know that it is 419! You see identity theft is an international crime occurring all over the world including Africa. Many Nigerians call many Nigeria operations 419!

We all have gotten those letters in our email promising friendship of sorts and a too good to be true investment scheme, proposals, and allegedly real business opportunities! African-Americans be aware of 419!

I thought the love we spoke of was real when there was time we were in daily contact

However these days I wonder was she just a 419 Queen! I know without a doubt that 999,900 out of a million single women in Nigeria would have welcomed a hand in marriage of an African-American man like me said many Nigerians to me but I gave this one lady every opportunity from my point of view to show me what type of woman she was and this is the story from my point of view! Maybe you can tell me if this was a 419 Queen or the real love gone badly or a little bit of both! Good bad or ugly this episode of my life found me writing some of my most private love poems I emailed and never intended to publish to my fiancé at that time in Lagos, Nigeria! However in telling this story I gathered them up from scratch pads and from emails in my sent boxes! I told this story about my relationship of sorts with this young Nigerian woman and my experience in Nigeria during my 2005 trip to Nigeria because my Nigerian friends made sure I had a good time! And my Nigerian friends in Nigeria told me that my fiancé was a fake maybe I should have listened to them and washed my hands clean of her right there in Nigeria! Write me by going to the email button at http://www.lovingblackwomen.com/ or write me at ljredd52@aol.com and let me know if this was a 419 scheme Queen or a real love gone badly on my Facebook.com fan page!

Introduction

Poet, writer, and school administrator I sat in the principal or site leader's office and dreamed about returning to Nigeria and writing again about my Nigerian connections. A good Nigerian friend introduced me to his niece in Lagos, Nigeria. The relationship blossomed online, through telephone conversations, and through letters.

For the first time in 24 years, I traveled to Nigeria to meet my lovely fiancée, Ese. While I wait and go through the visa process for her, I write poems professing my love. She is younger than I. Eventually, Ese receives a visa after four years and my young fiancée arrives only to get cold feet and returns to Nigeria or where ever.

While in Nigeria, I fly to Benin City with Ide Eguarbor and then we traveled 80 miles upcountry to a village called Ubiaja in Edo State, Nigeria, where I run into twin politician friends whom I had not seen for 24 years. What a reunion! These brothers Ide, Akhere, Odion and Ukali share 24 hours of conversations intensively! Ubiaja is the hometown of all these guys.

Long Distance Love is a travel narrative and memoir-love story about a struggling writer-school administrator determined to marry young Ese. My first autobiographical work was *Journey to the Motherland From San Francisco to Benin City*.

This book is a about the life, views, experiences, writings, true stories and reflections of a very interesting brother from inner city San Francisco through text, prose and Spoken Word style poetry. It is a story about long distance love, travel within Nigeria, and the reflections of an African American comfortably finding and enjoying our African roots in Nigeria and in America within his reflections!

When you read this book, you will enter Nigeria, see a relationship from beginning to the beautiful middle until its bitter end.

Larry Ukali Johnson-Redd

Table of Contents

Section 5

Section 6

Section 7

Section 8

Section 9

Remembering Chinwe
(September 19, 1952 –May 31, 1985)

I cannot think of Nigeria during the time I lived there without thinking of Chinwe, my late wife who was with me in mind and spirit every day I was in Nigeria.

Chinwe made most of my meals while I lived in Nigeria. Chinwe was born in Madison, Wisconsin. Her father and mother were in the USA during the time that Nkrumah (late President of Ghana) was studying in the U.S. in the early 50s. Her three brothers were also born in America, Her three younger sisters, however, were born in Nigeria.

Culturally speaking, Chinwe was 100% Nigerian by conscious choice. As a woman and wife, we felt it was her duty to fix my meals, like an African woman in Africa feels it's her duty to make her husband's food. Unless we went out to dinner in one of many Nigerian restaurants or to one of our friend's houses, Chinwe always made my food. Every now and then I would cook something special like spaghetti or hamburgers or even chili made from scratch.

Chinwe was a native of Nkwerre. In Iboland, like most of Nigeria, your roots come from your father. Chinwe's father (RIP) was from the Uzoma family in Nkwerre a village town in Imo State.

When she and I arrived in Zaria, in November 1977, her brother and sisters, father and mother welcomed us into their home. Mr. Uzoma, my father-in-law; had earned his Masters of Science in Biology while in the USA. Chinwe was attending high school in Lagos at Queen's College when the Nigerian Civil War broke out. Chinwe managed to get back to meet her family, in what was to be called "Biafra." Chinwe lived out the war in the war zone. After the war, Mr. Uzoma took his family up north to Zaria to help build the peace in Nigeria. Mr. Uzoma was a great biology teacher.

After the war Chinwe and eventually her brothers, who were born in America, came back to the States. I met Chinwe in San Francisco where she was attending City College of San Francisco. She eventually graduated from San Francisco State University. We met at a Nigerian party in San Francisco. My father-in-law suggested we say we met in a library whenever the subject came up in his hometown, jokingly, but we knew he meant it seriously. We fell in love, and the rest of the world disappeared.

I always knew she was down with me no mater how many changes we went through so I married her in 1974, December 20th.

When Chinwe and I arrived in Zaria for the first time, she slept in her sister's room and I was assigned to share this huge room with her brother who was fifteen or sixteen. We had our own room in Kaduna about 75 miles away but we had been married about 3 years so. I wondered what was going on but I went along with the flow.

The next morning I spoke with her father—man to man. Mr. Uzoma was a nice and pleasant man and Anglican by religious preference. Mr. Uzoma understood African-Americans and whites in a way most Nigerians did not know unless they had lived in America. He told me that although I was his daughter's legal husband, according to U.S. Law and even Nigerian Law, I had not yet completed the traditional Nigerian marriage, called the Native Law and Custom Marriage.

My father-in-law explained. He said that unless I do the Native Law and Custom Marriage, he would be severely looked down upon in his native village of Nkwerre. He and his wife could become social outcasts in Nkwerre if Chinwe and I slept together in his house without having completed customary marriage. We must sleep separately in his home at least until the traditional marriage and the elders of his village had drunk the wine. Until then, our marriage would not be complete in the eyes of Nkwerre and Iboland. This is the way it was in Nigeria, very cultural in its moral foundations.

Well, we completed the Native Law and Custom Marriage in Nkwerre in 1980. Sensing we would soon leave Nigeria, we drove our car from Benin City to Kaduna in 1981, during the Easter break or early summer after school was out. I was a Government teacher in a Benin City High School. We left when school was out of session in one of our two cars. We had a Volga that looked like a long 59 Ford; although it was made in the 70s and a Volkswagen Beetle that Chinwe drove to work.

When we left Benin, we headed towards Auchi. Auchi is in the northern part of what was then Bendel State and probably is now a part of Edo State. We passed a giant cement factory that operates 24 hours a day, seven days a week. When we were not reviewing maps and directions or talking about road safety, we talked about my school and students or her job as an education officer in the Bendel State Ministry of Education.

Somewhere between Ilorin, capital of what was Kwarra State and Minna, capital of Niger State, Chinwe fell asleep. So here I was driving in the middle of Nigeria. Besides my lights, it was pitch black.

I remembered an African Brazilian Brother I met in Benin City. He was a soccer coach. He was a very nice brother, but I do not remember his name. He had lost his wife in Nigeria in a crash while traveling. He told me a car was left in the middle of the road and he ran into it and his car landed in a ditch killing his African Brazilian wife.

Just as I was thinking of that situation, I noticed a vehicle right in my path. I moved over easily and luckily for us I missed that car and continued on to Minna, which was then in Niger State. We stopped in the motor park and bought gas or as the Nigerians called it petrol.

We got directions and a full tank of gas and headed for Kaduna City, which is in the next State to the North, Kaduna. Clearly another danger on these Nigerian roads at that time before the Nigerian Highway Patrol was established was a car passing on a two-lane highway. These days Nigeria builds four to eight lane highways, I am told. We continued on the Minna-Kaduna road until we got to Kaduna and then we knew we only had 75 more miles to go to reach Zaria.

We reached Zaria and found my father-in-law's house on the school campus. Once again the whole family came out to greet us. Her brother was gone. Chi Chi, as we called him, was en route to the USA. The big room was empty and my father-in-law said, "You and Chinwe will be here, pointing to a big room.

You see, since we had completed our Native Custom Law and Custom Marriage in Nkwerre, Imo State, and the elders of this Village had drunk the wine, meaning we had married by Ibo tribal customs, and in literal terms, it was now okay culturally and morally proper for me to sleep in their house in the same room with my wife.

I immediately fell into a deep, deep sleep after our 800-mile journey through the middle of Nigeria. Although we rested the first day, my father-in-law, Mr. Uzoma and I had hours of conversation. As classroom teachers, we told teaching stories about me introducing Government as a subject during the military government's administration until 1979. My father-in-law, Mr. Uzoma, had many stories about living in Madison, Wisconsin in the early 50s, life in America, life in Nigeria in Iboland and in Zaria. I also heard these stories of classroom experiences. Mr. Uzoma was a master teacher. You could tell by his professional and academic manner.

Mr. Uzoma had prepared for our visit by purchasing a case or two of Nigerian beer. It was Star Beer and 24-large bottles were chilling in the fridge. We drank so much while sharing our conversations that one of Chinwe's sisters started ranting and raving saying, "Dad, you don't buy beer like this normally." She then let off a loud hiss that was disrespectful. Mr. Uzoma ignored the hiss focusing on me with his charming smile and continued telling stories that revolved around how he taught students who had trouble learning Biology. I realized Mr. Uzoma was a master teacher, as a senior teacher on Nigeria's highest pay grade, like 14 or higher. I also told many stories about growing up in California and my teaching stories.

Mr. Uzoma and I lounged, drank beer, and told more stories between meals for two days. On the third day we began to prepare for the journey back to Benin City. We stayed three days and headed back to Benin City by car.

We reversed our directions and managed to see areas during daylight we had passed on the way. We passed many private mines in Niger State—Dave's mine, Michael's Mine and John's Mine—the real informal signs would say in the middle of Niger State. Chinwe and I wondered aloud about what these mines contained and what was being taken out of Nigeria and at what costs to Africa?

We passed the 24-7 Cement Factory in a fully lit up section of Auchi on the way back to Benin City. We arrived back there in time to go to bed. I was sleepy most of the weekend. On Monday I returned to my school. Many times during school we would report to school if we were not on vacation.

As I drove up to Eghosa Grammar School, I parked and got out of my car. As I emerged from my Russian Volga, I noticed six Benin-Edo teachers who were on my school's staff. The oldest of the group came to the front of the group as though he spoke for the group.

He asked me if it was true that I drove to Zaria and returned by road. In a fatherly voice this gentleman spoke, saying loudly, I am a Nigerian, born in this Benin City. At which point the other five joined in stating where in Benin area they were born. Then the older staff member began speaking loudly and the other quieted down. The older guy said, "We were born in Benin City, here but we would not ever drive by road that far in Nigeria because it is too dangerous on Nigeria's roads.

They then said individually, Thank GOD you returned safely. We all took turns shaking hands as we walked over to the staff room.

The Brothers were showing me a hearty welcome with a strong dash of caution about life in Nigeria in Benin City, Bendel State-Nigeria, West Africa.

(Read my other book on Nigeria a paperback titled Journey To The Motherland, From San Francisco To Benin City for a deeper analysis of Nigeria and my 4 year journey from 1977 to 1981 available at Amazon.com for 5.00 plus shipping at this link)

http://www.amazon.com/Journey-Motherland-Francisco-Benin-City/ dp/0967422639/ref=sr_1_1? s=books&ie=UTF8&qid=1366060925 &sr=1-1&keywords=Journey+To+The+Motherland+from+San+francis co+to+Benin+City

Remembering Felix Ide Eguabor

I met Felix when I first arrived in Benin City. It was when I moved to College Road to my crowded duplex apartment in the Ekenwa area from the Edo Guest House on Apakapava and New Lagos Roads. It was a small 3-bedroom apartment. This was a great improvement over living in guesthouses and hotels. Chinwe and I decorated our place and made it cozy.

Felix was a new higher school graduate and so I was a little older than he was. But Ide turned out to be a real good friend. Ide showed me around Benin City. We would charter taxis for two or three hours at a time and drive around looking at the ladies and the rest of the city.

We became good friends and I met his father and mother in their beautiful three-bedroom house in the Ekenwa area on the other side from the College Road area. I also introduced Ide to my late wife, Chinwe.

After about 1 year or so we moved to 3 Jemide Drive about four or five blocks away. The house we moved to was great. There were three bedrooms, a front yard, a small back yard and a one bedroom and bathroom in the back, called house help's room in Nigeria. My school continued to pay three fourths of my rent and I paid the other one forth of the rent.

The compound had another house twenty feet away. Most of the time I got along well. Sometimes I had to draw the line with Omoh, my Itsako neighbor.

I also set up all four of my huge speakers and played music, mostly reggae, loudly when relaxing or entertaining my friends or our friends. I will never forget our house at 3 Jemide Drive.

Ide Eguabor got a job at the *Nigerian Daily Times* in 1978 and he relocated to Lagos to become reporter with that newspaper. Ide would return to Benin, but we never had the time to hang out like we did initially. In 1979 Ide wrote the article I summarized in the front of *Journey to he Motherland*. The article was published originally in Nigeria's *Spear Magazine* (1979).

I wish I could hear from Ide Eguabor again so that we could catch up on twenty years.

I had two other friends—the twins, Ahkere and Magnus. I think their last name was Ugbesia, I hope I spelled their names right. These brothers were Ishan from Ubiaja in Northern Bendel Sate, Nigeria. Ahkere was a TV newsman, anchoring the news nightly in Benin City from 1978 until I left at least.

These guys were very good friends and we spent a lot of time together in their places in Upper Mission area of Benin City. Magnus was a university lecturer.

I traveled to Ubiaja with Ahkere a couple of times and we drove up into the mountains so he could show me his area. The Ugbesia twins told me they studied in Chicago, Illinois where the both graduated from one of Chicago's universities.

We were friends until the day I left Benin City, so it would be great to see or hear from the Ugbesia brothers again.

There are so many more interesting and exciting areas in Africa that I would liked to venture out into, such as parts of Africa that are not spoken much about here in America. There are many people here in America that will probably never be able to finance a trip to the Motherland, the home of the creation of life. They will read only stories that others have written. They will be able only to dream of touching the soil of our great and wonderful continent.

African-Americans and others are so hungry for the dream of Africa and information about Africa. After talking with people who have never been to Africa, I noticed that questions are thrown at me like a running river. For instance, my sister Sharon would often ask, how is the weather there on a daily basis? Is the air full of the sound of Africa? Are there streets there just like the streets we have here? Is the food the same and the people? What are Nigerians like in Nigeria, in general? I have also heard many stories of corruption. It is so obvious or is it like every country with only a few individuals who try to avoid the system?

To have photos of Nigeria was so very important., She wanted to see a picture of the street I lived on, I remember receiving letters from her asking me to take pictures of the inside and outside of the house, the roads and trees. Africa can be captured through camera and writing. If I go back to the Motherland, I will definitely purchase a good quality camera to take many, many pictures of the city, rural and unseen areas of Africa.

I really wished I could see a movie based on my book *Journey To The Motherland, From San Francisco to Benin City*, made by Danny Glover or Spike Lee or John Singleton or even all three of them. A movie of this type would close the information gap about Africa in the minds of African Americans and most white Americans as well as people of color in America and the world. There are streets in Africa with stoplights just like here. Why do we have to wait until Stephen King does it?

My life in Africa was the most meaningful and eventful time in my life. In the four years I lived in Nigeria from 1977 to 1981, I cannot count the number of times that a Nigerian walked up to me and spoke their native language to me thinking that I was a Nigerian. Other times, I was saluted only because I was an African American..

There was concern for African Americans expressed by well meaning Nigerians. I will never ever forget the great hospitality the Nigerians as a whole bestowed upon me. I remember the rough edges of some of the bureaucrats I encountered. But the hospitality of the general population outweighed by far the bureaucratic challenges. I will never forget the many times I appeared on Nigerian television in Benin City and the beautiful people of Benin City.

More than 400 million Africans around the world must continue this world wide African conversation.

Thoughts from Larry Ukali Johnson-Redd
From the National Interest Newspaper October 2005

Larry Ukali Johnson-Redd is simply a bagful. His name is Afrocentric in Look. While his progenitors may have been slaves to a Mr. Redd some 400 years ago, Larry finds comfort in his traditional African middle name, Ukali.

A GOD of mercy has equally been kind to this African American. His looks. Nothing about his looks suggests he is American. His oblong face, his crossbreed nose and those thin and silky hairs on Larry's head all combine to give him away as a Nigerian of the Fulani stock. This resemblance is complete when he tries to smile, and he does smile always. Those slim-chiseled set of teeth, they are unmistakably Hausa-Fulani.

At first contact, Larry Ukali makes an impression on you. He is full of life, always himself, he has honed his American accent so well it has obliterated the derogatory Black American slang that is ever seeing for shortened version of every word. In the course of the interview which followed our initial meeting at the office of the Editor-in-Chief of this newspaper. Mr. Johnson-Redd uttered the word 'gonna' just once. Amazing.

Another surprise is that Larry pronounces traditional Nigerian names and places with a finesse that will leave many indigenes hiding their faces in shame. From Zaria, Benin, Nkwerre and 'Kedu' the Ibo word for 'How'. And the sweetest Ibo words in the mouth of Larry are Chinwe and Uzoma.—names of the author's late wife.

These skills were not acquired in the backyard of San Francisco, Larry's home in America. They were learned on the streets of Benin City where the activist lived for four years from 1977 when they first came to Nigeria.

A glorious 24 years has passed since Ukali left Nigeria. But, he is back again. This time, he is not groping in the dark about where he should go or not. Even without the company of a wife, Larry can find his way about the town. And, he says this is a greater Nigeria that he has returned to. Larry spoke with Dennis Onwuegbu in his Hotel room in Lagos.

Excerpts:

Welcome back home, Larry. What brought you this time?

I came back for a couple of reasons. One, I haven't been to Nigeria for 24 years, I have a vacation and there is one young lady I want to have further discussions with. Those three reasons are uppermost in my mind. More so, this is an opportunity for me to write *Journey Two*. A sequel of sorts to my first book. *Journey to the Motherland: From San Francisco to Benin City.*

Compare with the first time you came to Nigeria, what difference is there now?

The biggest differences I've seen so far I how I entered the country. It was so easy and so sweet the way I flew in. I got off the jet and I was whisked through customs, they didn't do all of the humiliating searches like the first time (nearly 30 years ago when they went through every bag from A to Z). They were just wonderful.

So, now you don't have to worry about your privacy invaded.

And everybody was very polite and before I knew it, I was in Ikeja. Customs was a breeze. That means they want people to come to Nigeria and I enjoyed customs and I enjoyed coming into a Black country and being welcomed properly.

Would you attribute this to democracy or something else?

I thought to myself, given the way I was coming through Customs, so easily was but the fruit of democracy.

Not much is heard about American writers after great names like Robinson Jeffers, Waldo Emerson, Emily Dickinson, etc., What Is Happening?

We are there. Recently, we had in San Francisco the first annual African American Spoken Words Festival that was at the San Francisco Public Library on September 30th. The efforts that we make as writers are small because the publishing giants, still don't publish Black books in the main.

What has happened is that technology has blessed us now we know how to publish ourselves. And so, you have a proliferation of African American writers either publishing their own books or small African-American publishers publishing their books.

You are writer, who publishes you?

I'm a writer, but my books have been published like this *book History to Destiny Through Afrocentric Poems*, which is 303 pages of real hard Afrocentric poetry is published by Amen-Ra-Theological Seminary Press of Los Angeles. A very tiny publisher but very effective one. Again because of the progress in technology and our use of it, we know how to publish our own books now, even though the American big publishers ignore most Black writers.

How is the Black American response to Black literature and reading, generally?

Again, we still suffer from lack of exposure. So, once we publish the book, we still have to work hard while maintaining our jobs to promote the books. Again, I've noticed more and more young Black writers producing books, marketing books, but we are not getting chances to get on Bill O'Reilly or the O'Rielly Factor, we don't get chances to get on the national programs, we don't get chanced to get on a lot of the local programs.

But, where we have our own media, such as radio, like you have Global African Peoples Radio.com coming out of London, you have

LIB Radio dot com coming out of Los Angeles, you have the Atlanta Power Talk Radio dot com, so Blacks are invading the media through the Internet and through whatever chance we can get through with our ideas, publications and with our books. But we are meeting a lot of resistance from racist Whites.

Given the scenario you have, is it possible for an African American to be a full time writer?

There are a few who are into fulltime writing like Maya Angelou, I think there is one Mr. Mosley at the Los Angeles, there are several of them who are Black writers who have crossed over, as you call it and have White publishers who publish and promote their works. But we still face the obstacles (for small press) of the National book chains; they won't let our books in. I'm talking about the Barnes and Nobles, the bookstores that have coast-to-coast outlets; they seldom let Black written books in.

They'll give you a lot of reasons why they can't deal with small publishers and small press, lots of excuses. But I know for a fact that there are a growing number of young Black writers, who are promoting and producing their own books and getting books out there. And these people are going about spreading the words, giving positive examples to our youths and to people in our community about how we can empower ourselves.

So, it's a mater of time, but it's still pretty bad that in the most modern republic in the world, you still have such racist ideology predominating and ruling things. And so, you have two issues: What they do to us? And what we do to ourselves?

Blacks need to read more of the books written by Black writers and need to buy more of the books and products produced by Black people. That needs to happen. But, on the other hand, as American is the most so-called forward thinking democracy and the leading country in the world, they owe it to themselves to cleanse themselves of this white racism; so they can see the African-American for what he really is in his positive contribution, his intellectual capacity, and his abilities and that hasn't happened yet.

How then will you describe the reading culture among Blacks?

I think there are lots of Blacks who prefer other forms of media like DVD and CD and that's why Black writers are also making DVD and CD's to promote what they have to say. And, I do note that African-Americans read a lot. They have a large reading market. But this reading market is not recognized by a lot of the corporate book chains. And White Americans read very few books written by Black Authors. And, as long as you have that kind of divide, because we read both White and Black books on our side. but on their side, they never ever read our books.

And, they never ever read our books. And they never see our books, because when they go to the chain bookstores, they won't see our books. So, to a lot of White Americans, Black writers don't exist. And, that has to change for their good and for our good.

In dealing with your own books, from "History to Destiny Through Afrocentric Poems to "Journey to the Motherland", what has been the response?

Well, again, before my Black publisher published Journey to the Motherland, I sent my book to between to 50 to 60 White Publishers' and they all returned it with the same words: We don't want this kind of book. There is this kind of block in the minds of Whites toward what African-Americans have to say, which Whites have to get over because this world is becoming smaller. And, through technology, if they don't let these barriers fall, we goanna break those barriers, any way. We are coming forward.

So for your books, how would you describe the response?

When African Americans have a chance to buy our books, they buy them. Even White Americans buy them when they see them, at times. But, there is a lot of growth that can be accomplished in that area.

Of course the books sales for Black writers are minimal. They are not enough to sustain us as full-time writers, that's why we have to keep our day job.

And with this, I could better know how to help Blacks get along with each other.

In dealing with your own books, from "History to Destiny Through Afrocentric Poems to "Journey to the Motherland", what has been the response?

Well, again, before my Black publisher published *Journey to the Motherland*, I sent my book to between to 50 to 60 White Publishers' and they all returned it with the same words: We don't want this kind of book. There is this kind of block in the minds of Whites toward what African-Americans have to say, which Whites have to get over because this world is becoming smaller. And, through technology, if they don't let these barriers fall, we goanna break those barriers, any way. We are coming forward.

So for your books, how would you describe the response?

When African Americans have a chance to buy our books, they buy them. Even White Americans buy them when the see them, at times. But, there is a lot of growth that can be accomplished in that area. Of course the books sales for Black writers are minimal. They are not enough to sustain us as fulltime writers, that's why we have to keep our day job.

What efforts are you making to make your books available in Nigeria?

I am trying to get the books serialized here in the newspapers. I will not be able to publish the book here, but I am looking for a Nigerian Publisher who would like to make this available to Nigerians because the book is based on my four years journey in Nigeria and it would interest Nigerians.

In fact, in America, many of the people who buy my books are Nigerians and they love it. They want to get a realistic picture of what happens to an African-American brother when he goes to the Motherland.

What informed your choice of Benin City?

When I arrived here back in 1977, first, my late wife Chinwe Uzoma, had her parents living in Zaria so we tried to go to Zaria, to Kaduna so I could be a teacher there but for whatever reason things didn't work out there. So I decided to choose to go to another place and since the federal policy says you could go to East, West or Midwest, we chose to go to Benin. Again, there is this wise African saying that you never live in your wife's village. Benin was close to her area and was neutral to me. And, I know that Benin City is a crossroad of all the ethnic groups in Nigeria. And no one group rules it, and I wanted to e there to find out how Blacks get along with blacks in Africa. And with this, I could better know how to help Blacks get along with each other.

They never ever read our books. And they never see our books, because when they go to the chain bookstores, they won't see our books. So, to a lot of White Americans, Black writers don't exist. And, that has to change for their good and for our good.

In dealing with your own books, from "History to Destiny Through Afrocentric Poems to "Journey to the Motherland", what has been the response?

Well, again, before my Black publisher published Journey to the Motherland, I sent my book to between to 50 to 60 White Publishers' and they all returned it with the same words: We don't want this kind of book. There is this kind of block in the minds of (Some) Whites toward what African-Americans have to say, which (those) Whites have to get over because this world is becoming smaller. And, through technology, if they don't let these barriers fall, we goanna break those barriers, any way. We are coming forward.

So for your books, how would you describe the response?

When African Americans have a chance to buy our books, they buy them. Even White Americans buy them when the see them, at times. But, there is a lot of growth that can be accomplished in that area. Of course the books sales for Black writers are minimal. They are not enough to sustain us as full time a writer, that's why we have to keep our day job.

What efforts are you making to make your books available in Nigeria?

I am trying to get the books serialized here in the newspapers. I will not be able to publish the book here, but I am looking for a Nigerian Publisher who would like to make this available to Nigerians because the book is based on my four years journey in Nigeria and it would interest Nigerians.

In fact, in America, many of the people who buy my books are Nigerians and they love it. They want to get a realistic picture of what happens to an African American brother when he goes to the Motherland.

Interview with Larry Ukali Johnson-Redd

Author of *Loving Black Women*

By Rudolph Lewis

I've just completed your new book *Loving Black Women* (2006). It's packed full with a lot of heavy ideas and beautiful women. You have numerous photos of beautiful sisters, old and young ones,

some big-legged gorgeous sisters. I wish you had put their names in captions. I get the feeling from the content of this book; you don't know any ugly sisters. Or you just don't care to consider them. Is that right?

Hello Rudy. To answer your question I have about 200 female cousins in the San Francisco Bay Area, L.A., and Little Rock as well as across the country in my estimate. I contacted about 40 female relatives and those in the book are the responders. Thank you for the compliments for my mom, aunts, sisters, cousins, and nieces. Their names or relationship appear on the acknowledgment page in the front of the book. I truly believe every sister is beautiful from the beginning; however, some display ugly manners and that is the only thing that can make a sister ugly. Thank you for the compliments of the Black Women I loved all my life.

You lost your beautiful wife some years ago. Have you remarried or you just wandering in the garden, playing the field, so to speak?

Chinwe was truly beautiful and passed on when we were 33 years old. Much as I loved Chinwe I had to move on to stay among the living. I got married to a sister from Pittsburg, Calif. Named Sharon C. in 1990. We married and divorced in 1990. Since that time I have been involved with several different relationships with sisters from the US and Africa. As always I look for the for real love! However I am now ready to settle down with the sister I am engaged to hopefully within a month or two.

Have you noted, or is it just my imagination, that more men and women are living alone and in separate households than at any time in the history of Black America? You sing about loving black women—but are black women really loving black men? Or are they sort of hung up on themselves and their Oprah problems?

You have observed the same issue I have observed from the other coast. Many relationships between our sisters and brothers face challenges some because we are in a country where we are still treated like second-class citizens. Some sisters use the laws against brothers because they can. And sometimes brothers abandon their responsibilities because their money is not enough or shaky economics from the white supremacy state.

However, despite our situation as a people we have not had as much trouble staying together at any time as we are having now. Yet most of our sisters are and continue to love Black men. And if brothers and sisters continue to nurture positive relationships we help make sure we continue to exist as a people in the USA and the world.

So Black women love Black men in general. However, there are sisters and brothers who have issues. And we as a people and as individuals need to sort out our relationships and do our best to be great lovers to each other. As long as that happens we can face the challenges posed by white supremacy or the modern era with strong relationships.

I have written poems like "Love Your Smile" and "The Beauty of a Sister" to celebrate the love we Brothers have for our great Sisters! All of the poems in *Loving Black Women* are written to encourage love among us as a people so we can work together better for our progress in our relationships and as a people.

We hear women using such language as "booty call" and "being serviced." Where's the love in such language? It seems for many black women the black man has been reduced to his penis or in these more liberated times, his tongue. So when you speak of "love"— are you speaking of "erotic" love? Or of some kind of fantasized revolutionary love? Can you speak to these troubling issues?

This is a deep question that goes to the heart where we store our love. The language of "booty calls" and "servicing" speaks to the different types of relationships we are involved including single's issues. Some ladies have decided to stay single! I know sisters would prefer the whole relationship including marriage when they are with the man they love. However, that is not always possible.

So when I speak of the love of a people the ethnic glue that holds a people together, we are losing it and in the cases where we kill each other in the street we have totally lost it.

So we need to restore the people's love that Bob Marley called "ONE LOVE" so we can work together to survive in the current world we live in. One love that we need is not fantasized revolutionary love, but the love we need to see that will bring down the brother to brother killing we see in dramatic numbers in the San Francisco Bay Area, LA area and in the streets of the USA, the Caribbean, and Africa.

The other love you spoke of an erotic love must be nurtured as a part of a loving relationship to really be meaningful. I might have thought a little less about that a few years ago. I have written "Black Women Dear" and "My Dream," "Dialog with a Black Woman," "Pay Attention" and more to provide readers with a chance to reevaluate and improve relationships.

My impression is that the love you speak of is infused with a kind of Black Nationalism that excludes other races. There are black women with white male lovers and white husbands and half white children. Does that disturb you? And there are black men with white female lovers and white wives and half-white children. Do you think that those kinds of relationships work counter to the "liberation struggle"?

Clearly, at least to me, we as African people in America must reevaluate the love we are showing each other all over the world and all over this country we live in as a conscious priority. Any people put in the vice grip of white supremacy like us in America will have strained relationships.

Police and prison guards who place Black men and women in prison cells help stir up tensions among us resulting in fights that go back out to our communities. If we had the strongest love we could have as a people, we could not be so easily manipulated against each other without the deadly results on the streets of our communities.

We see too much of and attend too many funerals of young brothers particularly. My approach is we as a people need to look inward first to seek solutions to brother-to-brother killings in the rural and urban areas of the USA and throughout the African world.

I am getting married shortly and resent anyone telling me whom to marry. I am not personally telling anyone personally who to marry. I, like many African Americans, have someone in the family in an interracial relationship or marriage.

The relationships that should be of primary importance to us as a people are our internal relationships with each other as a people. A person that is so deeply involved in self-hate and political oppression needs to show self love as a conscious priority. If we can get through or to the establishment of ONE LOVE for ourselves we might even find it easier to love others. However, love like charity begins best at home!

There are more Hispanic and Asian men and women who are digging on black men and women. Should they/we be ashamed of such liaisons? Is this too a betrayal of the "black revolution" you envision?

Again the highest priority we as a people must be the self love and generating more love among us as a people serves our greater good and does not present a threat to anyone. So whomever someone chooses to love is personal. However, if we choose someone else because we hate ourselves, we will not be a good mate to any one including ourselves.

In *Loving Black Women* (2006) you call for an All-African Peoples Conference. In your concept of "African," you include peoples from Australia (Aborigines), Asia (Papua New Guinea), the Pacific Islands, the Middle East, as well as the Americas and Europe. Aren't you stretching African identity beyond what it can hold in practice and reality?

In the Middle East you have many Black-skinned people who choose their religion or national state as the focus of their identity. So an All African People's Congress may or may not appeal to that group. The other areas mentioned have African people as residents who probably would want to participate in an All African People's Congress as it is developed from an idea to a proposal.

I am speaking of African residents in European countries. New Guinea a country of Black-skinned people like the people of Fuji and other Pacific Islands, probably descended from Eastern Africa in some distant ancient time. It would be their decision to participate in an All People's Congress or not. I hope they would participate.

But I feet the Melanesians should be included along with Africans and Afro Brazilians, African Americans as well as other Black populations throughout the West. This is a thought and a proposal. However, the African people throughout the world must embrace the concepts of an All African People's Congress before it will ever become a reality.

I hope we will have an All African People's Congress in three to five years or at some future point in time in Africa, like Nigeria or Ghana, to assess what we can do as a people to assist each other to improve ourselves, to trade with each other, to develop people-to-people, political, and cultural relationships.

You seem to think that solving the identity question leads automatically to the resolution of larger problems like neocolonialism, poverty, ignorance, and disease? Do you think you are being rather fanciful? I mean isn't all this rather a fantasy?

When you travel to Africa as an African American you are immediately impressed with the power African people manage and exercise in Africa. I also feel that the young brothers and sisters in the streets and schools need to see how we can empower each other as well through seeing our leaders coming together from around the world as a realistic empowerment model we can implement in our communities around the world.

Sorting out and establishing our identity is but the first step and you have listed other issues we need to sort out and solve.

I do not think ideas like these are fantasy for Marcus Garvey and Malcolm X expressed these types of ideas in their time. However, we as a people have the power to make our plans and dreams a reality if we want to.

You worked four years in Nigeria as a teacher in the 1970s. Your Nigerian wife then worked for the government. It was your first time in a black country. You felt at home? Except for some government bureaucracy problems, you play down any other criticisms of what was/is happening in Nigeria. There must be something wrong there for we are finding more and more Nigerians desperate to leave their country to come to America or go to Europe. Can you give us now the real deal?

Nigeria is currently at once an independent country and a neocolonial state with progress and potential. The Nigerians battle the IMF and Western multinationals who tries to take advantage of the high-grade oil produced by Nigeria's land and costal waters. However, the Nigerians are well educated and could be the first African country to break out of the neocolonial status by developing to their full potential their resources of oil and natural gas as well as other natural resources, and Nigerian people.

These western companies are welcomed but do not act like good corporate citizens because they are driven by profits. So there are corporate challenges to Nigeria's independence. But the Nigerians are avid readers and very knowledgeable about their challenges and continue to make progress. Still there are many unemployed and uneducated hardworking young men and women in the country who want progress.

So Nigeria is the most populous African republic in the world. Nigeria is a third world country with first world potential and a dynamic population, As African Americans we will see hip-hop and other types of African-American influence in current-day Nigeria. For that reason I hope as many African Americans as possible can experience the good, bad and ugly that constitutes Nigeria so we can observe their successes and learn from their failures and see our people in Nigeria and look beyond western stereotypes of our people living in trees. I want my people to see the magnificent houses and regular houses our people live in Nigeria.

There are many young Nigerians who might like to come to the USA to study and settle here or study and return to their country to build up their country. Nigeria has a range of school opportunities but not every Nigerian can be in all of their schools at the same time

We know of three major tribal groups in Nigeria: Yoruba, Hausa, and Igbo. How much did you learn about these different peoples and the tensions that exist among them? Did your wife belong to one of these groups? Did you travel into all these regions? Make friends there in those regions?

When I arrived in Nigeria in 1977 the first Nigerian brother I made friends with in Lagos was named Abu—and he was a Northerner living in Lagos— the southwestern area of Nigeria and the commercial capital of Nigeria. Chinwe, my late wife, was at home all over Nigeria but is of the Ibo family of southeastern Nigeria.

I lived in Kaduna in Northern Nigeria the first nine or ten weeks. I traveled to the North, West as well as the southern area of Nigeria. I made the most and deepest friendships in the Benin City area. I traveled to Nigeria's East and completed the Native Law and Custom Marriage of my late wife's Ibo people.

I found it very easy to make friends all over Nigeria. However, there are internal issues that Nigerians must sort out for themselves. There are religious differences and tribal issues like there are problems all over the world. I traveled to Warri and Sapele in the Nigerian Delta like the American Gulf where you find massive poverty and multinational oil companies side by side.

You recently returned to Nigeria. You gave a half hour interview on Nigerian TV, talking mostly about the troubles blacks have in America. Was that the purpose of your trip? How did you find things different in Nigeria? Where did you go? Did you sell any books?

I recently returned to Nigeria 24 years after I left Nigeria with my late wife Chinwe in 1981. I found customs to be easier this time and the customs officer increased my visa from 10 days to two to three weeks, stating how you can't see Nigeria in only 10 days.

I was through customs so quickly I missed one of my friends who came to pick me up. There are many young Nigerians who might like to come to the USA to study and settle here or study and return to their country to build up their country. Nigeria has a range of school opportunities but not every Nigerian can be in all of their schools at the same time.

Rudy, I will always be grateful to you for publishing "Remembering Chinwe" in 2004, a short memoir that spoke about the last trip my late wife and I made to the North to spend with her family.

At the end of that essay I began remembering my Nigerian brother friends Ide Equator, Akhere and Magnus Ugbesia whom I had not seen or corresponded with for what was 24 years at that time.

That article was read in Nigeria and Britain by relatives of my friends. I got in touch with Ide, about five months before my trip. We traveled to Ubiaja and bumped into the twins Akhere and Magnus Ugbesia.

When Akhere and I met he was totally shocked and happy. We sat down and shared some beer and caught up on 24 years that beautiful night in Ubiaja, a village about 100 kilometers from Benin City. However, the primary reason I was in Nigeria in October of 2005 was to meet my fiancée and her family. I also looked for a Nigerian publisher. I am still looking for an Africa-based publisher.

You seem to believe that black-on-black violence is the major problem of black cities. Others seem to think that the major problem is the capitulation of black elites to white middle-class values and callousness with regard to the concerns of the working poor. Why such a divergence in emphasis?

I feel that both the brother-to-brother killing and the capitulation of some middle class African Americans are a part of the problem. The white supremacy status in America is the 800-pound gorilla. So our issues are very complex and yet there is more we can do to prepare to rule our world to rule our communities and to rule our destinies. May we all do more to reconcile ourselves, unite ourselves and liberate ourselves from the 800 pound gorilla.—White Supremacy—by working together to improve ourselves so we can develop ourselves until we are no longer victims of white supremacy.

You seem to putting books out as fast as Marvin X. How do you do it? Why do you do it? Doesn't your job as a professional educator keep you busy enough, already?

Please buy my books because writers like me who invest our own funds to produce independent books free of American corporate support deserve the support of African people all over the world that inform us about our issues and come from a sincere heart!

My books and media are available at some bookstores and my e-commerce equipped web sites accessible at lovingblackwomen.com and or journeytothemotherland.com. I have been busy writing Black Love Spoken Word, and presenting my Spoken word in the Bay Area, Sacramento. LA and any other community I receive an invitation from.

Please invite me and I will make a presentation in your venue. Buy your copy of *Loving Black Women* and *Journey To The Motherland, From San Francisco To Benin City* at my websites and I will send you autographed copies! I stay out of trouble by staying focused on working as an educator and completing my books and other media projects I have planned on for several years.

My books and media are my legacy. I appreciate and respect the work of our older brother Marvin X and appreciate being mentioned in the same breath by some one I respect like you Rudy! If you see Marvin X before I do please say ENOUGH RESPECT to Marvin for me!

You have been a long time supporter of ChickenBones. Why? What influence is it having in the Bay Area? Is there anything comparable to it, anywhere?

I am a sure *ChickenBones* draws attention from all over the world including the Bay Area. I know that there are many new online magazines but *ChickenBones* is the most popular and many of our folks and others from all over the world visit and cruise *ChickenBones* and we are all better because *ChickenBones* is available for us all! I keep in touch with the Black literary community by checking out *ChickenBones*.

Thanks ever so much for your time and your support. We wish you the best as educator, author, and performer.

First published *ChickenBones: A Journal* (24 June 2006)

Getting Ready

How do you get ready for a 25-hour plane ride if you have to go to work the day before you fly? You cannot waste time. You have to be early. If you are late, you could miss a flight. Your flight plan must be at the airport when you arrive two to three hours early to allow for the inevitable mistakes and still be allowed to fly. As an African-American man, you must have a checklist or your wife with you, or you will forget something very important.

I am on an American Airlines jet at the San Francisco International Airport. The jet backs away from the gate. The pilot announces the names of the crew and goes through the well-established safety speech.

I am on this flight thanks to my youngest brother Joe's good driving through Hayward to the airport. My brother reminds me of his earned master's degree anytime I give him big brotherly advice. My brother says it in such a responsible way that I remember he is driving me. So I shut up. I keep saying thanks for driving me throughout the drive.

Anyway, I continued to hope I've remembered everything as we roll down the runway for Chicago. I remember my days in the 1980s with Chinwe. I hope a mistake doesn't bite me. I remember the article Ide Equator wrote on me and my late wife, Chinwe Amechi Uzoma Johnson-Redd (1952 – 1985). May she continue to rest in perfect peace.

The article appeared in *Spear Magazine* in 1980 or so and made us famous in Nigeria. I used excerpts from that article to introduce *Journey To The Motherland from San Francisco to Benin City*. Ide Eguabor and I go back a ways. I lost contact by the time I left Nigeria.

I really have to say that I am apart of this world and have substantial web presence. All you have to do is go to www. JourneytotheMotherland.

com And check out my linked sites and all of the information at least 100 links.

It was my web site that put me in contact with Ide Equator or really it was my writing on *ChickenBones: A Journal* (nathanielturner.com). On my site I have had guest book sign-ins from Nigerians and Africans who saw my spread in Chicken Bones! Then Ide Eguator and I finally got together and traded some email reconnecting a friendship we had twenty something years ago. Several of my students from my Nigerian high school Government classes have signed in after cruising my articles and reviews on *ChickenBones* and then they have visited and cruised my website.

Through the internet and knowing powerhouse writers like Rudy Lewis, the editor of *ChickenBones*, Mike at Powerhouse Radio.com in Atlanta, the growing number of links from all over Africa, the world is becoming smaller.

As I fly to Nigeria, I think of Nigeria in realistic terms. Nigeria like anywhere else in this world is full of good, bad and ugly. But this visit is oh so special. I am meeting Ese Ohe after so much phone-to-phone and email communications.

We are finally going to meet eye to eye. I know we will hug and kiss upon our initial physical encounter in the Lagos Airport. We already know each other quite well in many ways. I am totally excited about meeting Ese Ohe Grace Momodu, her father and mother as well as other members of her family.

On the way to the airport, I stopped by Easter's house briefly in Hayward. I met Easter when I lived in Hayward. Now he is my friend. We talk on our phones all of the time. Easter is my buddy and Ese Ohe's uncle. Easter Momodu introduced Ese Ohe and me through several phone conversations. Easter is really cool and I will always be grateful for him introducing me to Ese Ohe.

I am still flying to Chicago so I can transfer to the British Airways flight to London and then on to London.

Suddenly, I begin to think about my job at a Bay Area high school and the kind gestures and words I received, as I was finishing out Quarter One of our block system. Assistant principals work with the principal as an administrative team in our districts. The vertical take off of the school year begins in August for students and staff. Among the kind gestures was a sister administrator giving me five CDs full of romantic African-American soul music.

My direct staff gave me a great looking frame so I could put my new wife's picture on my large new desk upon my return to the motherland. All of the encouragement from the principal and other assistant principals is appreciated. I owe them gratitude for working with me so I can have a chance to go to meet my wife after only working for three months. Now what a great group of professionals I find my self on the same team within my new school. I am truly a blessed man at this stage in my life.

I have a lot of thoughts in my head because I also begin to think of Katrina and the aftermath of Katrina. See all of my old and young mainly African-Americans still on the freeway, stuck at the Superdome and at the Civic Center. I saw hundreds plucked from roofs and rescued by boats on the water on TV news. It must have been terrifying, but especially for African-Americans moving to higher ground or designated locations only to be ignored by the government in Washington with the only agencies with the money and resources capable of responding to the crisis.

The whole world saw America at it's ugliest without a shadow or a doubt. George Bush was stuck on stupid. His aides proved to be incompetent. His administration's racism became obvious, allowing suffering seldom seen in the USA. New Orleans and most of its people were drowned in an orgy of blues, death, and government neglect.

Although I have a big desk after many years of being underemployed and a great job, the awful response to the aftermath of Hurricane Katrina was profound. If it had been in way Connecticut or Minnesota or even California, I am certain the response would have been different.

–The response to black broken lives was dreadful. The Red Cross also dropped the ball.

The presidents of Venezuela and Cuba responded with great sympathy to the suffering of the victims of the Hurricane Katrina. Here is a poem I wrote of the suffering!

Blame Game

Is it
A Blame Game?
No, It's real
A dam shame
You know what I mean
About New Orleans
After Katrina
Black Kings and Queens
My people
Demonstrating for relief
Help! Help! Help!
Is Bush a fool or a thief?
Katrina was a force
A deadly storm
That brought
The water and harm
But Bush
got stuck on stupid
Got my people
Hot and live
Days of waiting
On the freeway
Civic center
And the superdome
Dragging butt
George Bush
Oh George Bush
Where is the rush?
Of the storm aid
While my people die

Now everyone alive
Must ask why??
Day after day
Government negligence
Day after day
George Bush nonsense
And Condolezza
The George Bush Pleaser
Buying shoes while New Orleans
Suffering is in the news
And G. Bush
Where is the rush?
This makes us think
You don't like any of us Is it?
A Blame Game
No! No! It's really
A Dam Shame

Flying to Chicago

Well, I am still flying to Chicago so I have not yet arrived in Nigeria and yet I continue to have many thoughts.

I have to think about the media image of Africa promoted by Hollywood and other power centers of the American corporate media. CNN broadcasts to Africa and the world with a biased pro-American slant but unlike the totally right wing Fox Network. The Fox Network is a Republican Party mouthpiece. However, all of the pro government networks take pot shots at the Bush Administration for its poor response to the Katrina Disaster by the Bush administration.

After slamming the American media that continues to picture Africa only in terms of its disasters and wars, my thoughts return to the sweet young lady, Ese Ohe Grace Momodu, who answers her cell phone in Nigeria.

Ese Ohe Grace Momodu is very intelligent and speaks wisely way beyond her years in every conversation we have had over the last two and a half years and emails and telephone conversations as well as occasional letters.

When we speak my ears are filled with her beautiful voice. When I make good jokes, she laughs and when I speak seriously about political issues she listens and responds with follow up questions or she shares her experiences and opinions.

My book *History To Destiny* (2003), 302 pages of Afrocentric poetry, covered almost every subject relevant to the world. It included poems from over a 31-year period from the late sixties to late 2003. Although I recently received an award from the Los Angeles Black Book Expo, Oprah and her ilk of media tycoons and most American bookstores have largely ignored this book. My spoken word pieces continue to be thought provoking and descriptive of our Black reality in a modern and racist America.

I performed for fifteen minutes in LA without reading. I began to travel around the various gatherings of African-American thinkers, writers, and poets. In 2004 at the Tenderloin Book Fair, organized by Marvin X. I asked Loretta if we could do a spoken word show together, she said yes. We did it in San Francisco, June 24th, 2004. Although we had a lighter than expected audience at the beginning of the show it went on and got better by the end.

Loretta introduced me to Terry Moore, my brother poet and spoken word artist in Sacramento. I launched *History to Destiny* to a great audience, February 7, 2004.

Loretta and Terry memorized most of their spoken word poems and pieces and once I started reciting more than reading, I began to connect with the audiences. I could actually see the faces of the audience in a way poets who read could never experience. I met a lot of great poets in Sacramento from the Spit Fire to Easy Eric Goines and Super Nova. I met others as well in Sacramento because it is a real live spoken word set. Patricity Shadow was there as well as many Bay Area poets like Paradise and Marvin X. At that time Paradise appeared at the Java House every Wednesday night in Oakland, California, over on 14th and Alice. These days, I can recite my favorite spoken word poetry and pieces for twenty to thirty minutes without reading, offering a great interaction with the audience.

It was really crazy riding fifty to seventy miles up to Sacramento to present five to ten minutes at venues like the show produced by Terry Moore or some of his other productions at the Underground Book Store and even at Loretta's new spot at Gwen's Caribbean Restaurant. When I was at Gwen's my first job was to eat a plate of Caribbean food. In 2004 or early 2005 when I was a featured poet for Khiry Moore who is Terry's brother at the Sweet Fingers Jamaican Restaurant, I filled myself with tasty Jamaican Jerk Chicken. Then performed 25 to thirty minutes of spoken words, thoughts about Africa, and spoken word sister praise poetry.

In 2005, Saturday June 4th, I co-hosted a technology conference and Keidi came up from Southern California and gave a blazing one-hour presentation on emerging technology such as I.P.T.V. and challenged the well-attended event's audience to get ready for the window of opportunity that would open with the emergence of new technology. I gave a presentation on my website but I got challenged by the San Francisco Public Library, technology and learned that I cannot do everything well.

Finally, September 3rd arrived for the First Annual Spoken Word Festival at the San Francisco Public Library's Koret Theater. Although we sought to get the word out including a two-time ad donated by the *San Francisco Bay View* Newspaper. Thanks Willie and Mary Ratcliff.

I continued to call Ese Ohe on the weekends and sometimes mornings also. You see Nigeria's time is eight hours ahead of Pacific Coast time. So if I called by midnight, it is be 8 am the next day in Nigeria, unless one has to factor in daylight savings time.

Ese Ohe Grace Momodu is the sweetest young lady on earth despite her difficulties in getting her visa but she never took it too personally as an affront by the U.S. government. I look at it a little differently because I know that US foreign policies favor giving visas of all types to people who are white or apply from the white countries of Europe.

The September 3rd Festival of Spoken Word featured Carl Winters, the Kalimba King doing spoken word and three down knowledge, wisdom and roots from his book of poems. I met Tony Moses 25 years ago when I first returned from Nigeria. Tony Moses interviewed me many times on his KPOO FM Radio Reggae Program along with many other KPOO DJ's. I was even interviewed by the station manager J.J.-Next came La Rue as she presented new poems and dialog from her pains of a rough childhood to her development as a Caribbean Black woman in white America.

There were also about 10 open mic participants. But Marvin X abandoned many of the pieces he intended with a diatribe and statement about the African American and other victims of Katrina and government neglect since we were all still fired up about the suffering of our people we appreciated where Marvin X was coming from. The two MC's Eric Goines and Wanda Sabir were right on it.

We had a good crowd but not standing room only. Next was my time but like any time you appear in an event you have organized your presentation time is cut short to make it work. My brother Swig from KPOO and I recited about 10 to 15 minutes of my stuff from History to Destiny to my newly published book of sister praise poetry titled "Loving Black Women". I have fully developed Loving Black Women but started on this new Journey

This picture was taken after the 2010 San Francisco Kings of Poetry Festival

Flying to Chicago

I am still flying to Chicago; I am about an hour away according to a flight attendant who walked by. New, we are told by the pilot that we are beginning our decent to Chicago. I will have a 3-hour layover in Chicago and then fly; from Chicago to London United Kingdom or England.

The lady next to me finally says I hope you get paid by the hour since you have writing steadily since we left San Francisco. I responded by saying, I hope I get paid too but I am trying to write as much of this novel-memoir as I can in real time. She then returned to her conversation with her husband and the Fatal Legacy Book she was reading. Patricity and Shadow closed it out like only a husband/wife team could. I featured at Underground books, September 18, 2005 in Sacramento.

I performed with Terry Moore, He Spit Fire and a number of open mic Spoken Word artists. I missed having the LSB Band, and Scratch or Leon Gray: the keyboard player in my video presentation of spoken word done at Underground Books in Sacramento, their great music. Take an hour and go to my web site link placed here and hear video clips of my Spoken Word done 8/5/07 in Sacramento and one done in San Francisco 1/19/07 at Alexander Books! Obtain the deeper understanding!

I did many of my favorites, I have memorized and since there were women of color as well as white women present I tried out a new piece I have written. Called "The Beauty of A Women". This could be described as a cross over poem of sorts but folks love it.

Terry wrote me along email stating that GOD was blessing me with poetry and applauding my development as a performing spoken word artist. Terry Moore my brother thanks you very much, for your encouraging words!!! You are definitely the standard bearer for the spoken word artists in Northern California.

So now we are finally moving and descending into Chicago and I am locking up my pen for now. I have bought a five-subject note pad to write this book the old fashion way to really get the story as fresh as I can!!!

They woke up with their little breakfast. I am now a passenger on British Airways. The airport in Chicago is so huge that you have to go up and down the escalator walk more than a mile and still take trains at least 1 long stop. So once we entered the British Airways 777, a huge jet. I found myself seated next to a Nigerian Madam—wife and mother of 5 on her way to Nigeria for a Vacation of sorts to her area of South Western Nigeria. This Nigerian madam spoke of her five children and husband in Texas and her professional work life there.

Flying to London

Suddenly a British-type voice comes over the radio and says we are at 39,000 feet and near the Irish Coast. We are slightly ahead of schedule and in 40 or 45 minutes we will land in London Heathrow Airport.

We were awakened with coffee and one of the lightest breakfasts one could imagine. My watch says 2 pm California time. It is announced as 10 am in London. Time is messed up. However London time and Lagos time are one and the same

It is about time to stand on real land. I am headed for Nigeria through Ikeja. I signed up for a 25-hour flight. An interesting contrast, a couple of seats away are in western dress. Oh well!

The primary reason for my journey is to meet and marry Ese Ohe Grace Momodu, born or raised in Lagos but comes from the Esan (pronounced Ishan)-culture directly related to the Benin City, the -Edo tribal family and located 80 Kilometers or 50 miles north of Benin City..

We have exchanged photos and conversation. But now we will exchange glances, stares, kisses. And who knows what else, if the chemistry is right? The chemistry will be right, I conclude from our warm conversations and correspondence. However, some may think of this as a risky venture, I know Ese Ohe is for me a sure banker. Her father too is a very responsible Nigerian family and religious man and I have expressed to him my desire to be a great son-in-law.

Ese Ohe Grace Momodu is young, pretty and smart and I am ready to meet her upon arriving in Lagos, Nigeria. The table is set. But we will now arrive in London, experience a 3-hour wait, board another jet, and continue this journey on to Nigeria.

Well, I am finally seated on British Airways London to Lagos. I made a mistake. It was a 1-hour wait instead of a 3-hour wait. As we board the plane, we are 80 to 90 percent Black passengers headed for Lagos, Nigeria. Every seat is taken. I remember briefly that Nigerian Airways had flown me in before. Nigerian Airways only does domestic and maybe some flights to other African countries.

While in the ticket line, I met a Nigerian sculptor with full dreadlocks. He is living in Ikoyi, an area of Lagos however he is Ibo I believed. The gentleman gives me his card in a gesture of friendship. I greeted him in Ibo Kedu. He answered and was very surprised. Then he greeted me in Edo when I told him I lived in Benin City. The jet is full. I am sweating. The air conditioner is not on. My brothers and sisters don't complain, or say a word. It was hotter than the motherland. I set my watch to British time. It's nearly 12:30 pm. This is a 6-hour flight to Lagos. We will arrive at about 6:30pm.

Though we have yet to reach the Atlantic, I once again salute all of our ancestors who perished in the Atlantic during the horrible slave trade. Europeans and White Americans caused Africans to experience the Middle Passage..

I look forward to the end of my journey to Lagos and Ikeja, Nigeria. That thought is broken up by a flight official handing out landing cards that Nigerians do not have to complete. Oh Well! I quickly fill out the flight car., I wonder why I have to fill out a card for foreigners as I enter the land of my forefathers. Always there are more questions than answers.

The 747 jet starts moving. The air conditioner comes on, finally. At last I am headed for Lagos. It is October 2, 2005. Yesterday, I was flying away from San Francisco. I saw London but only for one day. I will return later and see more of London.

> Yes, I am inspired by our situations, to write. God gave me poetry, a spoken word. A lot of the poetry in my books I can recite for as long as 30 minutes without going into the book because they've gone into my heart and into my head. Poems like the Beauty of a Sister, poems like The First Bullet Hit. First Bullet Hit is a poem to try and teach Black people not to kill each other on the streets because of gang stuff and rivalry, because that is taking away a lot of our young warriors.

THOUGHTS, Pg. 33

Africa Bound

The world is round
But I am Africa Bound
I can hear the sound

And Blacks are found
Once again to
My Motherland
And always home
Of the Black Man
May my story be told
My homeland of gold
My people of old
Where it's hot
And rarely cold
Going in a family way
I will arrive
Later today
To meet sweet lady
Bound for African Glory
Flying past the Island of Gory
May my roots be found
I am African Bound
Hoping to see
A few old friends
Looking to see
Some brand new trends
On a jet full
Of beautiful Black faces
Taking off to Africa
Full of cultural basis
Going home to unite
With my Sweetie
Home, Nigeria I found
I am Africa Bound

Anytime I see a pretty woman,

I would wonder if she was as pretty as Ese. This feeling for a lady I have never been in the same room or space with was overwhelming. How much of Ese's outer and inner beauty could ever be properly represented in a photo?

My anxiety would be totally resolved in a few hours. I was all coming home. My excitement, nerves, and feelings were all over the place and probably so were hers.

Then a thought came into my head: Once I won Ese Ohe's heart, I would never ever be an underdog again. Winning Ese Ohe would make me a total winner. Ese Ohe Grace Momodu! I wondered if she would be in a dress, or wrapper, or jeans? I wondered if she would wear make up or not. Not that would make any difference. I wondered if she would respond positively to me if we would have the chemistry, you know?

Then I wondered about every thing all over again. I needed to take a break so I looked at the maps showing Lagos about 1000 miles due south of Madrid, Spain. We were 2000 plus miles from Lagos heading straight for Lagos. We would pass the ancient cities of Gao and Kano and run directly into Lagos.

We were 2 hours and 27 minutes from Lagos. We were over the mighty Sahara Desert. Gao is probably in Mali. We were down to 126 miles away as the clock went tick tock, tick tock in my heart.

We are cruising at 35,000 feet at a speed of 578 miles per hour. My heart is probably racing faster than this jet. I will put my pen down and try to chill out and calm down. I am still two hours and 20 minutes from Lagos. I will take a break.

A little later . . .

Still an hour and 24 minutes to go this is a count down. The map on the video screen is so very close to Lagos. We will arrive and go through Nigerian Customs in 1 hour and a few minutes or so. I would meet Ese Ohe.

Less than 1 hour . . .

I wonder if Ese is nervous or calm? I wonder how she looks, if she feels as good as I do about meeting.

I wonder if she is trying to chill out like me. I will not have to worry much longer! The closer I got to landing, the longer it took to get there. Until at last the British Airways jet full of beautiful Black men and women softly landed in Ikeja, the heart of the Mother Africa— Nigeria is for me.

When we landed, the British Airways staff was business friendly. We said goodbye and walked into the long hallway that led to two large tables. Two lines formed. One line was for Nigerians and other West Africans who are treated like Nigerians because of ECOWAS, Economic Community of West Africa States protocols. The other line was for foreigners or people from all other countries.

I joined the line full of mostly whites. I was joined by a Nigerian madam and married women who left their families to go to Ogun State for a six-week vacation. We sat together on the flight from Chicago to London, where she told me about her 31-year old-oldest son and four other children including boy twins, another son and a daughter. She had flown on an American passport but the Immigration Officer told her that she was in the wrong line so they moved her over to the Nigerian line.

I remained in the line for mainly white guys. Both lines moved right on along. In fact this was a completely new situation because it was such a breeze. Getting into Nigeria has never been easier. Maybe this new situation is the fruit of a civilian democratic government. I was asked how long I intended to stay. I said until the 10th of October.

The customs officer smiled and said try to stay for at least 2 weeks. He waved me on and I went to the next station.

I thought they would go through my luggage at some point. But I found myself going down a wide six-foot group of stairs where everyone was lining up around the luggage carousal.

I got a spot next to the carousal and looked at all of those who made the flight. Everyone was waiting for their luggage to start flowing out. The luggage started flowing and people started getting their luggage carts ready.

Parents grabbed their kids playing around the big luggage carousel. Suddenly my luggage appeared. I grabbed it, realizing I was getting mine before most everyone else. I lifted my luggage and rolled it to the next station. The next station lay on the other side of double doors.

Once I get through what would happen? I was thinking as I moved toward the double doors. I was greeted by a fine Nigerian sister customs officer in civilian clothes. I had only seen 1 customs officer in uniform. The pretty lady asked me for my baggage claim ticket that was a part of my ticket. She took the sticker and said enjoy your stay in Nigeria. I was suddenly out the door and out of the whole process.

Taxi drivers jockeyed and motioned for me to use their taxi. I looked for Ese to the east and the west. When I did not see her I relaxed on my heels not taking any note of the taxi drivers maneuvering. Suddenly a young male Nigerian approached me with a sign in his hand. The sign had my name, Larry, written on it. He said, "I am Ese's brother. Ese is right outside with my sisters." I felt completely at ease. Itua said he had a taxi. He requested for his taxi to be allowed in. I said hello and as we shook hands and hugged in a manly way.

The Volvo rolled up and we put my luggage in the trunk and I started entering the back seat owner's chair. Itua motioned for me to get into the front. I got in the front seat and we rolled out of the gate where there were suddenly more than 100 mostly beautiful women and a hand full of men.

Itua told the driver to slow down and move over right in front of three of the most beautiful women in the world. As all three piled into the back seat with Itua. The last of the three who got in was Ese Ohe Grace Momudu. The other two were her younger sisters (Anna, 21) and (Juliet or Obehu, 19). Ese Ohe, I could immediately see was shapely and beautiful in a way the camera was unable to capture. I looked back straining to meet Ese's eyes and said, "You are much more beautiful than any of your pictures. Awe struck, I repeated myself. She laughed!

Straining as she gave me a shy smile. Ese replied, "Hello Larry," with a gigantic smile and proceeded to introduce me to her sisters. Itua conferred with me which hotel I would go to and I said, the Airport Hotel. Itua repeated, "The Airport Hotel?" The driver had an immediate response, "I want two thousand naira." The taxi driver had slightly raised his voice but I didn't hear him. I was focusing on the beautiful African Queen sitting right behind me while trying to balance some luggage in the front with me.

We were in the middle of Ikeja a suburb of Lagos and people were all over the place all of a sudden. Nigeria like Iraq is not a place where birth control of any type is in evidence. It appeared as though there were hundreds to thousands of Nigerian at every corner and along the streets.

We traveled slowly about five miles and entered the Airport Hotel complex. Ese Ohe was so calm and beautiful as to be unbelievable or was it just me.

We got out the car and while I helped to move my luggage they took care of the driver and sent him on his way. We all went up to my room. By this time I was so hungry, I could barely see and so we ordered food from the room service menu while I took every opportunity to look and focus on Ese Ohe while remaining sociable with her brother and two beautiful sisters.

The intensive eye contact, warm embrace, tender kiss, the stars, and fullness of Ese Ohe were upon me.

We ate our food after my prayer and I was suddenly revived with my eyes focused on Ese Ohe Grace Momodu. I thanked GOD for my safe trip and the blessings of finally meeting Ms. Ese Ohe Grace Momodu.

Monday—Day 2 in Nigeria

Monday in Nigeria like anywhere else is when the workweek begins. I was up on my feet trying to figure out the money. Ese the African banker lady was dong her job. I asked for the cost of a bottle of soda pop like. It gave me the clue to figure out what was really needed to understand the naira. Not the naira of times before, but the naira of today.

The lady said the bottle of pop would cost 1.00 Naira. Huh, that means that the Nigerian naira despite all the oil wealth and other natural resources had suffered a 100% inflation rate from my last trip 25 years ago!

All of Ese's explanation and explanations of her brothers and sisters did not click on my lights in my brain until I remembered how many naira sodas I bought when I was in Benin 24 years ago. This one dollar orange drink brought home to me an understanding of how much Nigerian money, naira denominations had changed. The Nigerian naira of today is now worth 100th of the Naira of 1977-81. That would explain to me why I had seen Nigerian video movies where people exchanged huge stacks of money. On that Monday, the Nigerian government announced a 1000 naira note would soon be made available to Nigeria's bankers.

Monday went by so fast. Breakfast was complimentary at the Airport Hotel in Ikeja. I called my mother in Antioch, California, at a local Internet and business center a couple of blocks away. Itua, who is Ese's brother, helped me discover a barber in the area to cut my hair. We had lunch together and he was off to handle his business. I started buying newspapers and the *New Nigeria*. I made a couple of calls that did not come through so I found myself sleep early.

One thing I did on Monday—Day 2—was call my mom and let her know I made it safely to Nigeria, West Africa. I could tell by my Mom's tone of voice that she was deeply concerned and worried. I sought to comfort her and let her know her 53-year-old son was okay. However, even by this time I realized that Ese was exchanging glances with me. I spoke briefly with Keidi and Sparticus.

I also wrote emails to Keidi in Los Angeles, California, and Spartacus in London at Libradio.com and Gapradio.com respectively. Ese was shy but observant. We checked each other out.

I then sent an email to Ide Eguabor. However, my first foray onto the Internet produced mixed results because I could not confirm that the email I sent had actually been sent. Also I thought about how slow getting into the net was and how much faster I get there even when dial-up Internet service was to his DSL. I thought about Keidi comments about how slow my dial up Internet service was to his DSL. I thought to myself well, if Nigeria had dial-up, how much faster connections would be because in Nigeria you pay about $1.00 per half hour or 100 naira.

I then wrote Ide Eguabor an email but I could not confirm it was actually sent or received. I wondered why I did not see him at the Airport. Then all of a sudden it was time to go back to the Hotel and eat dinner. I left.

Tuesday, October 3, 2005

I discovered that the Airport Hotel was a total complex with most things you needed you could get conveniently within its walls, although you would save more when you moved out. I went to the Telephone Center within the Airport Hotel.

I called a lady to ask her if she would honor the Conversations on Africa Forum's first Micro Loan Program and be the first recipient to help launch the program. She agreed and said she had just left the Airport Hotel, Ikeja business. I met her in one of the hotel's lobbies and had a picture taken of the presentation as a photo opportunity for a small but growing organization with a large mission.

The Monday evening I took a taxi along with Kingsly Itua, Ese's brother, over to her family's house. I met her mother as well as all of the extended family, Ese was there but I could not help but feel the distance that I wanted so much to close. She smiled as we talked after all she was in her father's house.

Ese's father was at an evening church service but Ese and her mother had prepared egusi soup, my personal favorite, with more pounded yam than I could eat! This was a grand scale meal even when I took only half of the pounded yam. The yams are boiled real well, then beaten with mortar and pestle until soft. Ese was so shy, a classy type of well-mannered young lady.

This soup tasted very good. I finished it and soon thanked her and began leaving the working class residential part of Surulere. Again somehow not yet feeling any real warmth from Ese but knowing from her smiles that she was in love with me right from the first time we met in the airport and at the Airport Hotel.

I returned to the phone center this time to call Ide Felix Eguabor. In *Journey To The Motherland, From San Francisco to Benin City*, Ide Felix Eguabor had written a 1979 Spear Magazine article on my late wife Chinwe and me. We had connected through an article I had written in 2004. This was a piece I called "Remembering Chinwe and Nigeria." a 12-page essay where I recalled at the end some of my long lost friends like Ide, as well as Magnus Odion Ugbesia and Humphrey Akhere Ugbesia. That piece was posted on *ChickenBones: A Journal*. I have developed a great online relationship with the editor although I have never met Rudy in person. *ChickenBones* is a major website with an audience of millions from all over the world and I found Nigerians always all over the site.

In fact, I received an email from Obehi Eguabor in early 2005. Obehi's email expressed her surprise that I had mentioned her older brother Ide Felix Eguabor in my article. It took a little while before we got in touch because Ide like me in my professional position is highly placed. We eventually exchanged emails and even phone calls. Ide told me he would try to catch up with me at the airport. He and his beautiful wife did arrive at the Airport. But after I quickly deplaned, ran virtually through customs, grabbed my bags and left. The several calls I made Monday to him were unsuccessful. The first emails I sent out from Africa did not work. I learned from the experience.

Tuesday's call to Ide's mobile phone was successful and I found out he and his wife barely missed me at the Airport. We talked a few moments and then he said he would meet me at the Airport Hotel in an hour to an hour in a half.

I happened to be on my way out of the phone center when I walked outside and ran into my buddy Ide. As real men do we hugged after not seeing each other in such a long time period. My brother Ide was suited and booted in a distinctive black suit and tie while I had an African outfit on. We saluted each other and left for the executive wing of the hotel where he wanted to introduce me to his good friend Raymond. His friend was not there, but there were people in Ide's delegation, several of his workers, and staff.

The Brother's Got

The Brother's got
The Brother's dances
And the Sister's got
We all need chances
To make advances
The Brother's got
The Brother's got
And the Sister's got
The Sister's moves
The Brother's got
The sisters got
Rhythm drops
From the top
From the top
With rhythm
And togetherness
To get good grooves
The Brother's got
The Brothers dances
The Sister's got
The sisters' dances
And we all
Need chances
To make
Advances
100 Dancers
In the same way
Keep it steady
Stay ready
The drums beat

And the dancers feet
Looks and sounds
So sweet
May every Nigerian
Benefit you see
From the Profits
from the Oil Industry
My Nigerian
People Compensation
To the whole nation
My musical
Lyrical
Spiritual
and mystical people
As Africans
Of one family
Thank you so much
For welcoming me
The brothers got
The Brothers Dances
The Sister's got
The Sister's dances
Let's take our chances
To make advances

Written 10/08/05

At 9:30am in Lagos, Nigeria to a fast African Beat Inspired by African Beat Inspired by African Dances

Touring Nigeria

We partied at night
All over Lagos
With old and new friends
We shared a toast
I left the West Coast
9 days ago
And the Special Food
I loved the most
Ran through Benin City
Nigeria defeated Zimbabwe
Moved on up to Edo State
Towards Ubiaja
Touring Nigeria
Checking it all out
One thing about Benin City
All the girls look so pretty
To a Kingdom in Iguebei
After 1000 turns
But first passed Ekpoma
And I thought of her
Then we reached Ubiaja
To Honor one of
Those gone past, true
And meet great old friends and new
Great friends
Church was a colorful screen
With a beautiful singing choir Flying to Benin
Riding from Ubiaja
Through Ondo and Ogun States
While the rain paid the water rates

We knew we were
On the way
When we reached
The Ibadan Express Way
Rolling back into Lagos
At the edge of night
Sharing a cheer to the end
With a very old friend
So many beautiful sisters
Of every shade
The happiness in this church
May GOD be praised
Touring a slice of
Nigeria, not so long
This is type of town
Should go on and on
Touring Nigeria
And Esan Land
Enjoying with my friends
To in the home of the Black Man

Sweet Nigerian Bush Meat

Hot pepper soup
And Bush meat
Tastes so hot
Tastes so sweet
Early morning rain
Tougher than a traffic jam
Watch out as your turn
Don't hit that ram
Go slow
In Lagos town
May my love
Be found
Where ever
I am is my Kingdom
In Nigeria
I enjoy my freedom
Black faces
On the T.V.
Black faces
On all of the money
On all of the bill boards
There is knowledge
In these words
And the Bush Meat
I see in Benin City
But also sweet
Pretty Lagos Ladies
Plenty for street

If you visit
Nigeria, West Africa
Beautiful sisters greet!
Enjoy sweet Nigerian Bush Meat

Native Blues

Native Blues
You must pay your dues
My hard rhythms
Hard and good times
Native African Blues
May all have shoes
Make your moves
Nigerian Women in the news
Life - no dey easy
But if you can see me
Living so free
In a Black entity
Smooth sounds
Our culture is found
In our Nigerian Villages and Towns
My home is found
Salute my Nigerians
Top to the Black bottom
As a Black Man in Nigeria
I got my freedom
I got my friends
Respect and recognition
Nigeria West Africa is real
This is no fiction
Dancers on their feet
And the sweet, sweet Bush Meat
Tough Nigerian brothers
Walk tall and strong
On and On and On
Where we have Native Blues

Everybody pays their dues
Some got no shoes
Read the dailies or look at TV News
Pretty minds and faces
In the Church in all aisles
Eye candy in all regions
Pretty Nigerian women's smiles
Taste Star and Guilda Beer
And about a sweetie
Have no fear
Enjoy this country!
Where soul and hip hop music
Are played widely
Where we are
Truly free
Enjoy Nigerian happiness
And some Nigerian Blues
Enjoy Nigerian Life
After, now pay some dues

Surrounded by 9 Cuties

I walked by the
Airport Hotel Swimming Pool
And I saw a sight
That could make man drool
I did not know
When their decision was made
I was suddenly surrounded
By many a babe
There was nine of them
And one of me
All were wet
And very pretty
So one of them
Asked what do you
Have for us
Although tempted: no lust
I did not have a song
So I gave them a poem
I recited 2 good ones
To the pretty and wet ones
They were dripping wet
And bathing suits you could
See right through
I was a little tempted too
I was happy to see
The young cuties
They were very comfortable
With their pretty bodies
They said they were 18 to 21
I had watched

Them in the pool having fun
And there they were
All shades of beautiful Black
Surrounding me in
Lagos you see
From all over Nigeria
They had no fear
And some wore G-strings
I could see
So I said Good-bye
This is no lie
With temptation
Upon me
I ran to my room
Chilled this afternoon
The Nigerian girl
Welcomed me to their world
Nine sweet cuties in
Bathing suits and G strings
They surrounded me
In our Black entity
Charmed by all nine
They all were so fine
They were Lagos Girls
And Nigerian Bush meat
They were definitely
Nigerian Cuties

Down in the Motherland

Down in the
Motherland
Home of the
Black Women
See the sister's
Beautiful our land
Driving cars
See movie stars
Moderating T.V.
Programs you won't see
Asking smart questions
Populating Africa our Black Destiny
Down in the
Motherland
Home of the Black Man
See the brothers
Walking and standing tall
Respect by the sisters
The brothers make the cell
See the brothers
Building up a Black Nation
See the Brothers
Down in the motherland
On our African land
Music of the Motherland
Played by an African Band
Such a vast
Expanse of country land
Densely populated cities
Teaming population on hand

Thick rain forest
Full of natural resources
Schools and Universities
With academically challenging courses
And the monsoon rain
falls upon the land
Producing the food
To feed Nigerians
Down in the
Motherland
Home of Nigerians
In our Motherland
Home of all Africans

The Girls Are So Pretty

The ladies are pretty
In Lagos and Ubiaja
The girls are so pretty
In our African City
When you arrive
In Sweet Benin City
You will agree with me
Cause the sweeties
Are so very pretty
In my Benin City
All over ring road
And the entire city
Happy taxis pick them up
What a pretty load
Down in upper Mission
And Sokpoba Hill
At Uniben
They are fine my friend
In Iguebei
And Benin City
The sister's are pretty
In our African City
All over Iboland
Touring Esan land
The women are Pretty
In a Nigerian City
In the Country
Or the City

All of the time
Nigerian sisters are so fine
In Benin City
Throughout Nigeria
The girls are so pretty
In our African City

Tuesday—Called Ide in the am

I got up Tuesday in the am showered and headed for the complimentary buffet. The daily buffet at the Airport Hotel is quite a spread of very rich food.

Itua, Ese's brother, joined me for breakfast. So while we were eating I asked him if I could go to Ese's job. Young 20 year old, Itua answered, "That would be a definite no!" I responded, "But that is a way I can win Ese's heart you know, go by there, and take her to lunch in a real nice place close by!!! Again Ese's answer was a polite, "No, they order out for her department but they eat in an office area only." In my mind these were hard conditions to win a young ladies heart.

Now the spread at the Airport Hotel was a great one for breakfast. The buffet spread consisted of chicken or fish stew boiled or fried yams, fried plantain. Eggs cooked to your specifications. But that was not all. There were stewed beans, beef pork (not me,, oh), and beef sausages. Along the other table were fresh bread, hot oatmeal, and cold cereal as well as two types of juice and sliced pineapples and watermelon too. There was a big tray of chicken. There was a bean cake called Moi Moi (my personal favorite). It was also left on the table in a significant amount.

When finished with breakfast buffet like that forget about lunch until dinnertime where a snack may do.

Well, after the meal I walked over to the Airport Hotel's Computer Center. Yesterday, I had visited a local Private Computer Center. At the computer was the prettiest chocolate young lady in the world. I forget her name, but she was a knock out and a charmer.

I wrote an email to Ese, and I could confirm that it was sent and received. Next I sent an email to Ide Eguabor my long lost buddy.

Then I went over to the Airport Hotel's Phone Center. On Monday I had not realized everything was located within the Airport Hotel complex at a slightly higher than outside price.

When I arrived at the phone center, I paid money to have Ide called and he answered. Ide Eguabor greeted me and welcomed me to Africa—Nigeria!!! He said he and his wife were in the Airport Sunday evening but had some how missed me.

Ide said he would meet me in the Airport Hotel. In about an hour Ide arrived at the Hotel, but I met up with my old buddy outside of the Adebayo Block where my room 330 was located. We met as old friends—Ide and I—with a handshake and Blackman's brotherly hug. It was like all of a sudden we were both 25 years younger like we both just came out of a time machine or something.

We went to another side of the airport hotel where his good friend had an executive suite and Ide continued to welcome me to Nigeria and we caught up on things—his kids, wife and family, as well as my late wife and more.

Ide had to get back to his job as Editor of a famous daily newspaper but he said he would send his driver over in an hour or two to show me around Lagos. There was a place or two I needed to go to and so he was off. I can not describe how great it was to see Ide!!! We could not really catch up on 25 years in a day but we put a down payment on it.

Later that day, I met up with Ide and we drove back to his home in the Apa area. I met Helen, his beautiful wife, and three of their four lovely children, including Loretta, Felix Jr. and Loretta. His daughter was away at school. Helen had prepared egusi soup. Egusi is a melon seed. Nigerians, my late wife taught me, use a soup thin thickener. Everyone who fixes egusi soup fixes it differently and any Nigerian that knows me knows egusi soup is my favorite African soup, followed closely by Abono or pepper soup.

I truly enjoyed Helen's egusi soup and the great conversation I had with Ide and meeting his kids, especially David. David and I had spoken on the phone when I called one day. It was getting late. Ide took me back to my hotel after my goodbyes. Ide made two promises: he would have a staff person interview me and he would see if he could get me an African Independence Television interview.

The second arrangement was concluded before we got back to the Airport. He assigned his driver Sumbo, a great brother, to take me to the AIT Friday by 6 am for the Kao Kari morning television program at AIT. Ide also gave me one of his extra cell phones to use. Things were looking up in regards to media exposure, not so much with Ese. Finally, Ide mentioned going to Benin City and touring Edo States.

I fell asleep as soon as I hit the bed.

Wednesday—Visits by Ese

I was fast asleep in my hotel room. Then there was a knock at the door. I could not believe it. What a surprise. I rose to my feet. I grabbed my slacks and put them on and braced myself.

Me: Who is it?

Ese: Me.

I opened the door, shocked and surprised but saying, I am happy to see you! Come right in

Me:

Ese: I have been trying to get in for 30 minutes. I arrived hour ago. If I do not leave right away I will be late!!

Me: Surely you can stay a few moments.

There is a warm embrace.

Ese: I must go right away but I stopped by to greet you.

Me: Well, please stop by anytime, by the way.

Ese: (Interrupting) I am sorry I have to go.

Me: Take care. Wait let me walk you downstairs.

I recovered and jumped into my bathroom and as soon as I got back to my room. Ese was a little nervous and said she had to go to work right away. Ese is such a beautiful woman that it's such a pleasure being in the presence even only for a little while.

I jumped into the shower because Dennis, a newspaper reporter from the National Interest, a Nigerian daily newspaper would be by for an interview. So I used the buckets in my bathtub the appropriate way and had a good shower. Next, I walked down the stairs (3 flights) instead of using the lift or elevator.

I greeted the brothers and sisters as I passed. Nigerians are big on greetings and acknowledgement no matter what time of day or night.

I arrived at the main reception, walked past the bookstore down past the travel offices and beyond the banquet rooms until I opened the door to the restaurant. As I entered I was greeted and shown a clean table. I sat down claimed my seat, got up grabbed a plate, and assessed the free breakfast complimentary for paid hotel guests.

Even though I thought about the taste treat I was about to eat, I also thought about Miss Ese who had paid me an important visit.

The table was full of food as usual. On one table was yam chips boiled and browned, cut in chunks. There was fried plantain or dodo, and moi moi, as well as stewed beans. I helped myself to a piece of yam, moi moi, made from black-eyed peas with out the eyes, boiled and steamed cooked into a bean cake. I skipped the stewed beans and ordered some hard scrambled eyes from the short order cook.

I got back to the table and skipped the pork and grabbed some beef sausage. I then went over to where the fish stew was and covered my plate with the fish stewed tomato type sauce. I sat my plate down and returned to the table for an orange drink and glass. I poured a full glass. By the time I got back to the table my scrambled eggs arrived hot and ready to eat. The food was fantastic!

I enjoyed my breakfast so well I skipped lunch.

I walked back up the stairs ignoring the lift or elevator so I could walk down some of my breakfast. I got back to my room and looked at CNN, BBC Lagos TV and Nigerian Television Authority TV, the nationally based Nigerian station.

A light rain began to fall and the phone rang. It was the front desk saying Dennis, a reporter/writer from the National Interest Newspaper, was at the reception desk waiting for me. Dennis was here to interview me. I returned to the front desk and shook Dennis hands and we walked out to the reception door on the walkway only to be greeted by the rain. We ran from the reception building about 400 feet to the front door of the hotel wing. I stepped in.

We took the elevator after greeting the security elevator and room service employees as well as other hotel guests. Nigeria is not a place to walk by people silently. Not in all situations anyway.

Once we entered my room Dennis a cool brother brought out a first class state of the art tape recorder put it on and went to work with his primary secondary and tertiary questions. (You have seen the interview at the beginning of this book).

Two hour later, Denis clicked off his tape recorder. I walked back out with him using the stairs to walk down to the street level. We shook hands again and Dennis was off.

The rain was over so I walked two blocks over near the swimming pool after I passed the gate. As a hotel guest—there no fees. I walked past the ping-pong tables and sat near the bar but where I could see the pool. There was a big Olympic sized pool. I sat there looking at the pool. There were many young girls in the pool this time. I also looked at African Independent Television and wondered why I could not get it on the TV in my room.

‘ Yes, I am inspired by our situations, to write. God gave me poetry, a spoken word. A lot of the poetry in my books I can recite for as long as 30 minutes without going into the book because they've gone into my heart and into my head. Poems like the Beauty of a Sister, poems like The First Bullet Hit. First Bullet Hit is a poem to try and teach. Black people not to kill each other on the streets because of gang stuff and rivalry, because that is taking away a lot of our young warriors. ’

◄━ THOUGHTS, Pg. 33 ━►

other in the United States. **Did you get this knowledge?** Oh Yes, I did. Benin was a city and you had Igbo, Itsekiri, at that time Bendel State and you had all the major ethnic groups in Nigeria represented in Benin City. And I noticed that everybody got along very well in Benin City. And that's where everybody spoke their broken English that's like a *lingua franca* and I picked it. I knew how to speak it when I arrived in Nigeria but I really got it much better when I lived in Benin City.

While teaching in school I spoke grammar but as soon as I got into Benin City, then it was time to speak some broken English. I really enjoyed myself and the way Africans were relating to themselves.

How will you describe Nigerians living in the United States of America? I will describe them as brothers and sisters, because when a Blackman goes to America, though he is from Nigeria, he might think first because he has a country then he has an advantage over the African American who don't have any country as such. But eventually, in the course of their stay, they are going to be beaten by the same White racism, that has beaten us for 400 years. When that happens, then the Nigerian has an awakening of his blackness in America than he would have had in Nigeria because in Nigeria they somewhat carry the White people somewhat on a pedestal. They think the White people here are so good and so great, but when they go to America they see what Whites can really do. Then they see a whole new reality. When the Nigerian comes back from America, they are wiser because they know more about what manipulations the Whites can do to hold blacks down.

What has influenced the simplicity of your book cover designs? In the first place, again it is simple. You want to get people to open the pages and if you put all the glamour and the stuff on the cover, that attracts people who are looking for glamour but a simple book you want people to go into what's inside not what is outside.

My book History to Destiny to Afrocentric Poetry, you can see it is red, black and green and these are the colours of the flag that Marcus Garvey gave to African American back in the 1900, 1914, 1920 and the Universal Negro and Prominent Association that Marcus Garvey started, the philosophy lives on. So the national colours of the African American and the African American flag is red, black and green. My books appeal to the patriotism of the African American for Africa and for African American freedom.

The contents of the books are alike – freedom for the Blacks, a radical approach to Black liberation? Was this influenced by your background while growing up or the conditions which you find Blacks in America today?

It is because of our on going situation. I have two centers degrees and a BA. So, I really don't have to suffer the same indignity as some of my people suffer. But, I feel it! And because I feel it, I write about it. And because I write about it, I'll promote it. And I promote freedom, and promote Black on Black love and I try to move people away from Black love and I try to move people away from Black on Black crime.

So, our destiny is in our hands. We have to be a more united people, both in Africa and in America. That's why my books try to push our people in the direction of more self-love and more unity and more working together so that we can better ourselves and better our situation. That's my whole purpose for writing.

What is the source of your inspiration seeing that you also have to keep a regular job? Yes, I am inspired by our situations, to write. God gave me poetry, a spoken word. A lot of the poetry in my books I can recite for as long as 30 minutes without going into the book because they've gone into my heart and my head. Poems like the Beauty of a Sister, poems like The First Bullet Hit.

First Bullet Hit is a poem to try and teach. Black people not to kill each other on the streets because of gang stuff

and rivalry, because that is taking away a lot of our young warriors. A lot of our young people are dying on the streets of America because there is fighting among ourselves.

My writing is coming out in prose but also more in poetry and spoken words. And the newest book again, Loving Black Women is about 80 per cent spoken words and poetry and 20 per cent prose.

And the next one for which reason I am in Nigeria which is called To Africa with Love; Journey II, is going to be in prose format but inclusive of poetry.

Does poetry get across to blacks in America easier than prose? Spoken word is very strong especially among our young people. So, when you speak to them in that format, they hear. And I go to a lot of spoken words venues in Sacramento, Los Angeles, up and down the West Coast. All over the United States there are places where spoken words are offered and young people come to listen to good conversations in a spoken word format.

That's a good way to communicate across age lines, across class lines, across all lines to our people who need to have that kind of communication the most.

Because, what they get from the American media is a glorification of murder and gangsterism. On TV, on BET you see gangster raps like 50 cents and some other gangster raps. And those guys I believe if they have a chance to talk sense to young people, they will do better job of it.

But they have to make commercial music and producers who call the shots, who are many times Whites will tell them if they talk something progressive in their spoken words or raps, that is not commercial. And so, they will block it.

Then you find groups like Public Enemy who try to be progressive, they find many barriers placed against them, then they don't become popular, they don't have their music selling much. So, they take the path of least resistance, make a song that says nothing make their money and go their way.

They forget that power they have to speak is to be utilized for Black liberation. They

don't see that because of the short term gain. So, one day we hope they will see that there is power in the spoken word and they will use that to bring progress to their people, not to bring more profit for some company.

There are also Black American publications, especially magazines, how does their impact on Blacks? First you have to look at the ownership question. There used to be Essence

magazine owned by Blacks, it has been bought out by whites; you have BET (Black Entertainment Television) that used to be owned by Blacks, it has been bought out by Whites, you have this Black clothing line. For us, again it was bought out, by a white company.

Now, you really have to look at what's really Black. See if it's Black owned, and if it's Black owned is it by Black people who really want to do something for the community

Tantalized and Tantalizer Restaurant

Oh, I did notice that the young ladies had on bathing suits of a skimpy type and when wet they were very revealing so you can imagine my smile when I noticed 98 wet young ladies suddenly surrounding and dripping wet and see through, right up in my face.

The young ladies asked me who I was and I told them, I had flown in from the United States of America.

Each one then gave me a welcome to Africa hug. My clothes were now as wet as their bathing suits.

So they introduced themselves with their hugs but I cannot tell you who was who. They were all young. I asked if they were 16 or 17 and they all replied by saying they were 18, 19 and 20, 21 or so.

Still they were standing all around me with their firm anatomy clearly visible. I admired all of the black beauty I could until they said what do you have for us. I knew they were thinking dollars and even maybe a little more. So I told them I had two poems for them. I recited "The Beauty of a Sister" and "Black Woman of Mine."

I looked these pretty young ladies in their eyes. Then I again asked their ages. They again stalled; they were 18, 19, 20 and 21 or so and left one by one and headed back to the swimming pool. I ran back to my room to cool down. The ranged from light to dark from thick to thin and from tall to short. All of them were young and fine and beautiful probably from most of the southern and or middle belt regions or Nigerian States.

I relaxed and called the engineer and asked to put African Independent Television on my television. The engineer was done in 20 minutes making adjustments in my room and in the Central Office. I now had African Independent Television in my room. I enjoyed ATI until the hotel phone rang. Reception said I had visitors waiting for me including Obehi and Ita. I knew it was Ese's brother and sisters.

It was about 3 pm. They suggested we walk a couple blocks away to the Tantalizer Restaurant.

I had been staying in the hotel complex that day so I walked with Ese, Itua, her brother, Obehi, and Juliet, her sisters, across the street outside the hotel, Awolowo Road formerly Isheri Road. After we got across the street, we walked down the street with the colorful taxis and many motorcycles of all types and the buses and jitney type vans and cars and pedestrians sharing the road African style. Then we passed sellers on the sidewalk hawkers in the street, moneychangers with wads of naira and probably some area boys.

We finally reached the Tantalizer Restaurant about one long block away from the Hotel. But it was a colorful walk that is for sure.

We entered the restaurant , a real cool site. There was a long wall at the opposite end of the restaurant with the menu written on it in full. There were two rolls of booths including tables where young people male/female were involved in meals or intimate conversations. There was a 32-inch TV at one end clearly visible to those who cared to see. The place was really nice and on the TV 50 Cent and other rappers by way of aFrench Hip Hop station called Tracer. This was the station I watched in my room. I ordered jolof rice and spicy chicken, a spin off of African-American barbecued chicken.. We all ordered our food and sat down. I said a short blessing and we were in the food.

The soul and hip-hop continued to play until my chicken and rice existed no more. The sisters ordered what I ordered but added a soft drink. I drank water. You must drink a lot of bottled water when you are in tropical Africa.

We walked around a little looking at markets and returned to the hotel. I saw them off and returned to my room. I went to the computer center long enough to send Ese a romantic email. Then I chilled out with one Star Beer.

The brothers got the brothers' dances

Among Nigerian artists are a bunch of new entertainers who were almost totally non-existent when I was in Nigeria 24 years earlier. This group was so well organized and professional in presentation that I was inspired to write "The brothers got the brothers dances." All 100 or so dancers had matching uniforms and highly organized dance routines. As their performance occurred teams of eight dancers advanced to the cameras while all of the others stood in place and kept the routines going while staying in place. I saw waves of beautiful sisters in groups of eight dancing to a hip hop beat thumbing. Then the sisters would move to their side in their cute little outfits while the brothers in a group of eight stepped forward.

The African-American Hip Hop proves popular in many of our videos were neatly worked into the Nigerian sisters' routines. There is a tremendous amount of cultural influence flowing between African America and Nigeria. This dance group offered a tasteful sample of the influence.

The routines of this dance group were at once definitely and uniquely African and even Nigerian, however, the African-American worldwide unity that inspired me to grab my pen as the dance presentation winding up.

There were many different Nigerian TV stations where African-American Hip Hop dance routines were worked into Nigerian Hip Hop Dance routines. In fact there is a booming Nigerian Hip Hop scene. I remember partying at a Lagos Hip Hop Club.

I also heard the "N-Word" being used as a way of relating to me however, since I do not use or condone the use of the 'N' word I felt that was not the best cultural influence to share with our Nigerian brothers and sisters. I hope every one in the African world will stop using the N-Word.

I can draw a comparison to the Area Boys of Modern Nigeria's urban areas and the African-American unemployed youth and young men who are locked into a life of a Black on Black Crime, violence and mayhem. In Nigeria and across African-American, African people must try to get jobs and job training opportunities for them to get them on the life sustaining and positive path not just condemn them for the negative activities.

Since I was on vacation, I spent some part of everyday by the Olympic sized size pool at the Airport Hotel. The DJ there would always play Hip Hop and Reggae as well as Nigerian Pop music again another expression of African-American music in our Motherland.

The young ladies in Nigeria have discovered thongs and strings so again, the African-American influence Nigerians in their expression of their fashions. The Nigerian sisters have always worn braids and they look so good with this traditional African style booth in Nigeria/Africa, the Caribbean as well as the USA. I know the sisters are wearing those African braids all over Europe and Canada as well.

So the African-American is well represented in good and bad ways throughout Nigeria and our Motherland. However, we need to look at what types of influence we want to promote or others will be in control of our image.

The Airport Hotel Complex

The Airport in Lagos, Nigeria is called the Mauratala Muhammad International Airport. This Airport is not in Lagos but in Ikeja an adjacent smaller suburb type satellite town like San Bruno is a suburb of San Francisco. The San Francisco International Airport is in San Bruno not San Francisco.

The British Airways Jet I landed in flew into Ikeja.

The Airport Hotel complex is in Ikeja about 10 miles from the Airport. I felt like I saw 100,000 to 300,000 Africans while riding from the Airport to the Airport Hotel.

When the taxi pulled into the Airport Hotel compound, I did really see the entire complex of buildings that support the Airport Hotel. However, I got around to the pool with it's bar TV and DJ playing Reggae, Soul, and African Music. The reason I use the word complex is in addition to the Hotel you have a phone center, a computer cafe, a barber shop, a book store and several other shops offices and banquet halls and rooms.

There is also a travel office and a business that will convert your dollars. There are also two car rental companies there where you rent a car and driver together as well as a section for taxis of a private nature. There are about 10 categories of Hotel Rooms from the Executive rooms and suites to the regular rooms, like the air-conditioned room I was in.

When there is a power cut or interruption in that area of the City of Ikeja, the Hotel turns it's own power plant on and life continues to go on normally.

This complex has a lot of security from one end to the other as well as a lot of staff.

I mentioned the spread served daily and called breakfast where I would eat until I was really full and skip lunch because I was not really hungry at lunchtime.

The free complimentary breakfast is highly recommended by me at the Airport Hotel.

The many staff include the guys who clean your room, elevator operator, banquet people in their colorful uniforms. The bar and room service people, the bar in the main reception are workers, the receptionist and managers and still many more like the maintenance staff and engineers.

If you are in Nigeria for the first time and you do not wish to pay $300.00 per night to stay at the 5 star hotel like the Sheridan Hotel if you read Journey To The Motherland From San Francisco To Benin City you know the Airport Hotel has a night club but this time I counted two night clubs.

One day I think it was the day the girls surrounded me at the pool. I noticed AIT Television on their T.V. I returned to my room but could not get it on the TV in my room so I called the engineer's office from my room phone, a young Nigerian knocked on the door.

I could also hear commotion and chanting of workers outside my window.

The engineer informed me that the workers were on a work to rule— like a labor dispute or demonstration, like a strike or slow down due to management walking out on a meeting when the workers' were presenting their case.

As I was informed the workers also turned off the electricity and blocked the plant workers from turning their alternate power source.

The issue was resolved if at least for the duration of my stay and those same workers went out of their way to make sure guests did not suffer.

Thursday October 5, 2005

Later, Ide Equator's driver Sumbo came by and took me out for a ride around Lagos.

I woke up early and had my bath. Then, I walked past the elevator and walked down three flights of stairs and I walked down the walkway past the guards and the check in—station.

I walked over the building where the reception desk was located past the bookstore and down the hall. You finally arrive at the restaurant for your complimentary breakfast that could last most of the day.

I sat down and looked around the restaurant. All of the various staff from the hostesses, to the cook, to the cashiers in uniforms well the cashiers had their own clothes, but most of the other workers all over the Airport Hotel had smart looking uniforms.

The spread of food was pleasing to look at and smell. I had a nice plate of food to treat myself as well as I can. That is what I always try to do you know—take good care of myself.

After I had eaten and washed it down, I returned to my room to wait. I knew this would be a meaningful day. Bring it own—bring on the day what ever I am ready you know!

I looked at African Independent T.V. for a long while. Then I used my remote control to switch past CNN, BBC to Nigerian Television Authority. I checked that out for a while they had an authentic Nigerian Drama Series on that was intense about inheritance. Then I switched to this French Channel. Although the announcements and commercials are sometimes in French, however, 90% of the music they is African-American Hip Hop almost like B.E.T.

The phone rang out. I answered the house phone and the reception folks. Say Ese and her sisters and brother are here. I said send them up. We took a chartered Hotel Taxi to Victoria Island and other areas.

When I returned to my room, I had my last mid day nap. After the Thursday nap, I stopped feeling jet lag—you know. Traveling great distances will have some impact on you, but you get over it when you make your adjustments with the right attitude.

I slept very well that afternoon at 5 pm or so Sumbo arrived and took me over to the National Internet printing facilities and office operations center. The staff people are busy as ever at 7 pm or 8 pm finalizing the morning or late edition for the next day. I finally get the tour by my buddy Ide Eguabor. The building had the energy of a home media beehive of positive energy with Nigerian professional journalists busy and focused on every floor of their building.

After the town tour, their best photographer took several shots and pictures of me for the feature article.

I came back wide awake and sat at the pool. I had a gulder beer. I listened to music being pumped out by the poolside D.J. A lot of reggae and hip hop turned up loud. Imagine that African-American and Nigerian Hip Hop playing loudly at the Lagos Nigeria swimming pool. I was feeling good in my neighborhood in our motherland Nigeria West Africa!!!

This place was a scene with young lovers in the pool, warm weather, suya or barbecued beef called Suya being cooked on an ongoing basis. Pepper soup available there also. Some young people are seating at the tables and chairs, some are playing ping-pong and some are playing pool.

I sat there and wondered if my people in the USA knew how popular we are in Nigeria. I wondered if we would ever know!!!

That big bottle was enough all by itself. I was headed to my room. Oh by the way, I would need to be up at 6 am for the ride to the African Independent Television Studio Friday.

I decided I would get up at 5 pm so I could eat my free breakfast before going over to the ATT Television Complex.

So I went to sleep but not before calling reception.

Ukali: Hello, reception

Reception: Hello Sir

Ukali: I need a 5 am wake up call.

Reception: Okay Sir!

Ukali: Can I count on that wake up call?

Reception: Yes Sir, I will be on duty and I will call you.

Ukali: Okay, thank you and good night.

Reception: Good Night.

Friday, October 7, 2005

I woke up at 4:45 am and I was seeing Lagos wake up call came through loud and clear. I thanked the brother on the other end. I took my shower and did what it takes my self-ready to go on T.V.

I had finished another great breakfast and picking my teeth when I ran into Sumbo in the reception area. It was 6 am. We walked over to my buddy's vehicle and left.

It was 6 am and I was seeing Lagos wake up realizing that many had not slept because like New York, half of the people work days and the other half work the night. We have a long way to go and not much time. As the light of the sun escapes the clouds I can see rows of neatly parked taxis and minivans filling up with passengers. We passed next some buses . We are passing through the heart of the hood in Lagos, Nigeria.

We drove through mostly working class areas. Man, all you can see this early in the morning are machines—motor cycles of all types. People are all over the place walking, riding taxis and some types of green mini trucks and mini vans I have never seen before.

We also see the street hawkers among the cars with household goods, boiled eggs, ice cold sprites and coco colas.

The traffic is now thinning out. We are on the edge of the city. We pull into a driveway. The huge doors open and we drive in. A few minutes later we park and go into the broadcast studio meeting, Brother Sola (pronounced Shola).

We are guided to a plush waiting room. There are other guests here in the meantime. It is now 7 am and The Kaakari TV program begins. I am the first or second guest. I am led to a comfortable seat on the set. The interview happens. I know how to handle myself most of the time. I was treated very well on the air and felt very comfortable while I was interviewed on Kaakari AM TV. You can see a 4 minute video clip or a 10 minute clip clip on You Tube if you type my long name in the You Tube.com search box.

Last week there was an announcement by the government announcing a thousand naira note. Many Nigerians applauded the October 12, 2005 introduction of the new note. When counting out 20 to 50 notes one becomes delirious or loses count. (You can see five minutes of this interview on my website.)

The hotel has a high-speed money counter to assist the cashiers.

Since my departure was short by two days on October 10, 2005 for their introduction of the new thousand naira note. I do not have any of them, however; I have plenty of naira in my pocket. Plenty of course is a relative term as Nigeria's currency has been ravaged by devaluation by the West and spiraling inflation. Imagine in 1981, I turned in my naira and for each naira; I was given $1.82 by the bank. However, now during this trip, I pay ine hundred naira for a sprite or coke instead of the one naira 24 years ago.

However, Nigerians have made the adjustment undaunted and unfazed by the situation. I feel though in my heart the Nigerian currency has been assaulted by the West to keep Nigeria from reaching its full potential and yet despite that fact and some mistakes by very wealthy Nigerians, Nigeria is such a dynamic country with such a dynamic population that Nigeria will meet its challenges head on and reach its full potential in five to ten years.

Ese's brother and two of her sisters visited but had not been able to see the interview because of a power cut in their home in the Surulere area of Lagos. They left as dark approached. They were always there you know very supportive and welcoming. Real Cool!

At 6:pm my partner Ide Eguabor came on by and we had a drink at the bar along with Suya. We caught up on some of the last 25 years but definitely not all that time could be addressed in a few days.

Finally, Sumbo picked us up and we were off to three or four nightclubs. We also spent some high quality time on a Lagos street when we had a flat tire. That took hours.

That flat took so long to fix that daylight caught us when I was dropped off. I had spoken with my friend Ese who had to travel suddenly. Ide said he would be back at noon to fly out to Benin City. A tour of a part of Nigeria, I hold dear, Benin City and Edo State.

Saturday – October 8, 2005

I slept three hours and I was up and checking out at 12 noon from my hotel. I saw Sumbo and soon Ide Sumbo and I were headed for the domestic Airport for a flight to Benin City.

We had a few moments of doubt, but Ide said we would be flying to Benin City. Sumbo would meet us in Benin City. I said okay brother let's do it. We boarded the flight but not without some hesitation at seeing how small the jet was.

Lagos was covered with clouds that were covering up the sky. As I put my seat belt on, Ide sitting across the aisle said don't worry he flies these jets all over Nigeria three to four days per week. The late great Kwame Nkrumah said the secret of life is to have no fear.

The Flight To Benin City

As I flew over the Nigerian country side I could see those tall trees and little villages where most Nigerians live in the rural areas.

However, you will realize that this is mainly an agricultural country on a flight like this. There are about 30 seats on this aircraft, probably built in Russia or somewhere in the old Eastern Europe.

You will not realize the rural dimensions to the countryside while in the middle of Lagos and there are fifteen million residents, and businesses.

I see Lagosians—all fifteen million commuting to work, selling retail goods, ready to eat snacks like pealed oranges, boiled eggs, complete meals, carried on heads or transports on wheels. In fact, on most streets one will see cars of all types, trucks, motor bikes, motor cycles, carts, truck pushers, pedestrians, policemen and police women, soldiers, traffic police, buses, vans, minivans of all sizes and street hawkers on sidewalks as well as street hawkers who walk among the cars on the road selling their wares.

As you roll down Lagos streets one will see restaurants, business companies, small factory outlets, hotels, bars, houses, apartments, share rooms and more.

I cannot stop thinking about how small this jet is. The rain is light though persistent. And we keep heading toward Benin City. I am writing to avoid the nervous feeling I have about flying in this little jet. Cloud level, we are in turbulence until fifty miles out of Lagos. We made our way through rain and rain clouds but we kept aloft.

I looked out of the little window at the farms, the fields filled with neat rows of, plants and trees.

I look down again and see nothing but palm trees and brushes.

The pilot announces over the speaker we are beginning our decent into Benin City. This is a fifty-minute flight. This is an associated airline flight flying out of the Nigerian Airways terminal.

During my first journey in 1977 to 1981 only Nigerian Airways could fly in Nigerian. Today they allowed competition. As always when I land safely, I thank GOD. So as we landed in Benin City, I thanked GOD.

We got off the jet and walked into the terminal a few feet away. We get a taxi and head into the historic and modern city known as Benin City.

As we drive into Benin City, we check out the modern developments. Then I started seeing some of those beautiful Benin City women of all shapes and sizes and shades on the streets.

I did not know what Ide was feeling but I was remembering how we rode up and down those streets 24 or 25 years earlier. Beautiful women continued to color the scene.

Finally, we arrived at this sports bar at the beautiful Saidi Hotel which was a new addition to Benin City somewhere in the last 25 years. Ide and I watched Nigeria's soccer team defeat Zimbabwe. Nigeria was not going to make it to World Cup 2006.

After the game, we met up with Sumbo and headed north over the Ikpoba River Bridge. We were headed for Iquebeis. We passed through hours of villages and two lane highways pass Ekpoma, where I thought of Ese and called her with a cell phone in Ibadan Oshun State. We spoke for a short time and we continued our journey.

After some hours later, we reached Iquebei and found Ben in his kingdom. Ben received us well and after touring his kingdom we had some abono soup, pounded yam, and bush meat in one of his dinning rooms.

It was dark now, so we headed for Ubiaja. We arrived in an hour and half. When we got settled where we would spend the night, Ide and I visited a couple of very great dear friends in Ubiaja. Since they are government officials, I will leave their names out, but these guys were doing great and we had a happy reunion.

Sunday in the morning, Ide and I attended services at the St. Benedicts Catholic Church to celebrate a memorial for his grandmother who had died a year or so earlier. We visited our friends and arrived at Ide's uncle's house for bush meat, pounded yams and abono soup somewhat different than we had yesterday. There are always many varieties of Nigerian foods. That Church was full of beautiful sisters. The singing was great.

We were now headed back to Lagos. We went back to Iquebei and joined up with Ben. Ben decided he needed to go to Benin City and we pushed on towards Lagos.

We saw rain most of the way but we had good cheer and good conversation as we rolled through the Nigerian countryside until we arrived in Lagos Sunday night at 7:30 or so just ahead of darkness.

We were all tired so Ide dropped me off at the Airport Hotel and I checked in again. Ide went home. I went to sleep in my hotel room.

Oh Africa

Oh Africa
Which one you dey
Oh Africa
This is our day
When will we
Unite for African People
United States of Africa
Every African treated equal
The power is in Black Hands
On all African Lands
One united Africa
On our lands and Islands
No more work to rule
Every African child in school
Every family, 2 houses
Every house has 2 browsers
So we must unite
When we feel it's right
For the destiny of the Black Man
Unite the African
May time finally come
Africa, unite and be number 1
Our ancestors will celebrate
When our work is done
Africa oh Africa
Which one you dey
Oh Africa unite
When the time is right

World Wide African Freedom
and the Million More Movement

Gain knowledge
To win
Gain wisdom
For freedom
This is not
Just any event
This is the
Million More Movement
Don't participate
In Black on Black
Genocide
Prepare now
And enjoy life's side
No killing each other
My sister and brother
We all need
To learn and read
Instead of killing
Each other
And seeing our people bleed
May we try harder
To get along with each other
Be right sister/brother
Prepare for freedom
Prepare for Liberation
Prepare to unite
The whole Black Nation
In America/Melanesia
The Caribbean

In Africa make real
Our free Africa Dream
This is not
Just any event
This is the
Million More Movement
Knowledge and wisdom
Is the key
Unlock the power
Of world wide African Unity
Gain Knowledge and wisdom
And we'll have African Freedom
Get wise
So we can rise
My might people
Arise
Embrace our
Common sense
Celebrate our African Essence
This is not
Just an event
This is the
Million More Movement
Open African eyes
When we get wise
All of our people
Will rise
Develop universal
African wisdom
And we will get
Our people's real freedom
This is not
Just an event
This is the million more movement

Flying Back to the United States

Ide came by at about 4 pm and we had a few more drinks at the swimming pool in the Airport Hotel. My jet would leave by 10 pm.

We checked in and headed for his place. When we arrived his wife prepared a feast for us and all his family was there to say goodbyes. However, we prayed and feasted on vegetable soup and jolof rice, as well as chicken and goat meat.

I was full and ready to go to fly back to the United Snakes of AmeriKKKa. I hugged Ide's sons and encouraged his daughter to complete her school in a very serious way. I encouraged his sons too, especially David but also Felix Jr.

Then we left driving back for the flight out of Murtala Mohammed International Airport in Ikeja, Lagos, Nigeria.

We arrived at the Airport on time and I said goodbye to my buddy Ide Eguabor, I also saw Itua, Ese's brother at the Airport and thanked him for all his help.

The British Airways jet loaded up and took off for London.

As I am flying out, I saw three or four European men showing off the African artifacts they were taking away Africa in a small area outside a rest room. As we entered the jet we could all see that there were about 90% Africans and maybe 10% Europeans. This British Airways jet is full of African people from all over West Africa by the dress, accents and outfits of men and women.

Malians, Sierra Leonians, Ghana, Nigerians, African-Americans and probably some Jamaicans or Caribbeans were there as well.

As the 767 or 777 taxied and took off, I had mixed feelings. I wished I could have spent more time with Ese and gotten to know Ese Ohe Grace Momodu much much better. This will be my biggest regret of this journey II. I mentioned I made a big mistake. I thought I left my shot record but I found the original and I found the copy when I opened my main luggage in my Hotel Room.

Although no one ever asked me for my shot record, it is a serious safety issue and I have been told that if you leave the US and return without having a shot record, that shows you have had a yellow fever shot you could face exclusion from the USA or face a period of time in a quarantine situation. I had yellow fever innoculation and a couple of other tests as well as typhoid and malaria tablets. You have to have your shots 30 days before you are ready to leave at least.

* * *

I have been back in the USA for three weeks. The envelope mailed to me has a copy of the interview I had on Nigeria's African Independent Television, an international and independent television network based in Lagos Nigeria,.. There is also a three-page interview in an edition of the *National Interest* newspaper.

Yesterday when I spoke to Ide in Nigeria, he told me that another Part Two had been published and he would mail me a copy.

African-American Influence on Nigeria

I saw a lot of African-American influence in Nigeria we may or may not be aware of. In most cases, we can be proud of our influence on our motherland. We must be concerned, however, about some of our negative influence on Africans and ourselves.

When I arrived in Nigeria many folks were talking about the Katrina Response or lack of it. Many said they will send their children to London for graduate studies instead of the USA because of Katrina aftermath and its obvious racism.

Nigerians know have full access to American cable through their television systems and the cable patch ins and hook ups. Nigerian also has full access to BET and to African-American hip hop through a French station that is all over Nigeria. When I walked into the Tantalizer Restaurant a block or so from the Airport Hotel I heard all of the latest African-American hip hop sounds as well as reggae and Nigerian contemporary musicians doing their thing. Although 50 Cent had left his mark during his tour, other African-American musicians owe it to themselves to do a tour of Nigeria and other African Countries.

One evening while I was watching (AIT) African Independent TV, I saw this dance group that made a presentation. They used a regular beat machine beat under the leadership of a poet/artist who appeared after the performance with a tam covering his dreadlocks, which are very popular now.

Ride To Africa Independent Television (AIT)

Television showed me how Lagos wakes up. Since Sumbo and I left for the AIT at 6 am exactly for the AIT, exactly. I saw Lagos without traffic jams, Lagos flavor—ladies, men, school kids—walking and getting buses, eating breakfast on the run, and heading for school and work.

By the time we got to the AIT at the edge of town I had traveled thirty or forty miles through the streets of Lagos that Sumbo knew well. We must have seen ten thousand street traders; selling everything you could and could not think of. We saw buses, vans, minivans, mini buses, micro mini vans, jitney types, taxis painted like taxis and many private cars that were used like taxies.

One thing for sure, among the hundreds, thousands an even hundreds of thousands of Lagos residents, I saw so many beautiful shapely sisters. I salute all of the women of Africa for their enduring beauty and loyalty to us African men. If you are ever able to see the interview, I did on Africa Independent Television, you will see the beautiful sister who interviewed me.

African women are very intelligent, and beautiful and play a powerful role in building up Nigerian Society by producing and educating its growing population. Nigerian women include many sisters who play their part in business and industry. When I toured the *National Interest Newspaper* offices, I was impressed with the intelligent brothers and sisters I saw handling their business.

Ese's Family and the Eguabors

I really would like to take this time to thank Ese Ohe Grace Momudu and her family as well as Ide Eguabor and his family for all of the great African hospitality I enjoyed while in Nigeria.

Ese's brother, Itua, accompanied me around some areas of Lagos showing me the sites. Thank you to the Momodus.

I had dinner a couple of times in the Eguabor's home and Helen, Ide's wife, is also a great hostess and cook. Ide and I flew to Benin City where he refused to allow me to pay for many things because this was his hometown. Then we drove up to Iquebei where our friend Ben has built himself a kingdom in Iquebei. We had a slamming abono soup, along with pounded yam and spirits.

The next thing we did was travel to Ubiaja arriving there around 11 pm at night. By midnight, I woke up my politician friend in the Ubiaja area. We were up til 2 pm talking and moving back and forward through 24 to 28 years of history from his law degree to my second masters and from his place in Benin City where we used to visit each other two to three times a week to my life in the San Francisco Bay area.

Ide and I drove back to one of his family houses of his extended family in Ubiaja.

We slept and attended the remembrance of Grandmother Eguabor who had been buried a year prior.

After that service we had bush meat in Abono site in his uncle's house. However, this abono soup was prepared differently than the abono soup and bush meat we had in Iquebei, about 15 to 25 miles from Ubiaja. Cooking styles in Nigeria have a lot of diversity.

Well, Ide and I had a great conversation with his uncles and his uncle's friends and one of his uncles spoke to me about living in Hayward, California for awhile. I lived in Hayward, California for seven years.

We stayed too long and ran back by my old buddies places and then back to Iquebei before heading to Lagos this time by road.

Nigeria Then and Now

Progress is a relative term and the expansion of western style buildings in Lagos, the commercial capital of Nigeria, is only a part of the way to analyze development in Nigeria and yet some Nigerians may argue if Nigeria has made as much progress as I saw.

Nigeria does not yet have uninterrupted power so high speed internet is not yet wide spread but Nigerians have grown up in the tech savvy department remarkably well. Nigeria has grown in the number of factories developed over the last 24 years. Since I left. the biggest change is cell phones. Cell phones are all over Nigeria where as 24 years ago there were no cell phones. The cell phone networks work very well through out the country.

Lagos traffic jams like New York City traffic jams are no joke. None of the cars is created, molded, produced, and assembled in Nigeria, though a very modern country overall.

Nigeria is a huge country full of mostly underdeveloped rural lands, but with a substantial urban section including at least fifteen to twenty cities like Ibadan, Port Harcourt, Owerri, Kaduna, Jos Kano, and Benin City with more than a million people.

Nigeria is the mother of all African countries population wise, set to play a pivotal and leading role in African politics as well as African world politics. It remains primarily an agricultural country yet reaps huge profits from the rich deposits of liquefied natural gas, more plentiful than the deposits of oil.

So Nigeria continue to grow, develop your economy.

And, people, may Nigeria continue to spread wealth to more of its most in need people. May Nigeria be enjoyed by the have and the have nots, in other words, the greatest majority of the brothers and sisters.

May Nigeria continue to keep the vision of African unity upper most in our African hearts so that one day we will all be proud to see a United States of Africa in a form that is consistent with our African people and our world wide African interest.

Old Nigeria, traditional Africa, has always lived side by side with modern Africa. We need to nurture our traditions and the development of modernity to the benefit of all Nigerian, all Africans and for African people all over the world.

May many millions, more African Americans and Africans all over the world, come to Nigeria and other African countries and reconnect with our beautiful African roots.

I filed my fiancée visa application completely December.23, 2005 with the INS—Immigration and Naturalization through the Homeland Security. However there was sixteen months of furnishing more documents, contracting with a lawyer. Ide suggested I ask for my House of Representatives person whose constituency services manager turned out to be a great advocate. And then more documents were required and lots of waiting. I also hired a lawyer to assist my efforts I wrote these poems while waiting all of those sixteen months.

Ese Ohe Grace Momodu

She has a
Million-dollar smile
Beautiful braids
Have my child
Ese Ohe is African
Consciousness
A total lady of
Sweetness
Coming from
Esan Land
Ekpoma
Land of the Black Man
Growing up in Lagos
Her eyes are pretty the most
But now she's in Lagos
I want you
In my arms
Your Smile
Contains your Charms
Meeting you was
Meeting your beauty
Hang on til I make you
My wife and sweety
Ese Ohe Grace Momodu
You better know
I really
Love you

To Africa with Love

Blessed by God above
Goodness is what
You are made of
To Africa with Love
Like a beautiful peaceful love
Sweetness is what
You are made of
Smile Ese Ohe and
Share my hug
To Africa Sweetie
With Love

Choosing a wife

Once in life
Or maybe twice
In your life
You got to choose
A wife your wife
Twice in your life
Or even thrice
In your life
You have to
Choose a wife
And that my friend
Is a real decision
That is a real choice
My brother, Ide my friend
Cannot be
Indecisive
Choose a wife
For your life
Pray for reason
From God for the
Right decision
Then go with the vision
This is your time
This is your life
This is your time
To choose your wife
Once in your life

Unite As One

As I think
About you
I want you by
My side
But you are so
Far away
From that I
Cannot hide
Soon the time
Will surely come
When our two souls
Will unite as one
So 'til then
Hold my pride
When we unite
We will enjoy the ride
I want you
By my side
When I meet you
You'll know I tried
My heart and soul
Refuse to rest
To unite with you
I will try my best
Oh my GOD may the
Day come
When our two souls
Can unite as one
A heart felt
Long distance love Affair

Is a special love
To share
That's why
I got to get there
To show you
How much I care
Our love is one
That is profound
Our love
Will be sound
Now my life
Is so lonely
You and I will
Love only
Soon the time
Will come
Our two souls
Will unite as one

Kill a Brother

Black Man
In October 2005
6 Shots 2 dead 4 Alive
Self inflected Genocide
Where is Black Pride
No one can stop us
If we self destruct
If we kill each other
Is that really so tough
Or is it others
Killing our brothers
In our community
Where is Black Unity
And the one love
Blessed by JA above
If a brother kills a brother
While oppressed by the other
Where is our common sense
Can we unite our African Essence
And come up with Unity
As we struggle for equality
Or will we kill

We are no longer brothers

In Oakland
Or Lagos, Nigeria
Our destiny is ours
Even in Liberia
Can we rediscover
Unity among a brother
Stop killing each other
Unity will take us further
Rediscover the one love
That unity is made of
Stop the murder Brother
So we can unite with each other
Cause if we
Continue to Bleed
Brothers will die
That we really need
Unite my Brothers
Please
With no Unity
We are on our knees
Let no hand
Kill our Black Man
Let the Black man
Stand in Oakland
Let a Black man Lead
Don't make a brother bleed
All over our Motherland
Let an African Black Man Stand

Long Distance Love Calling and calling

I don't get through
Then I really
Think about you
Calling and calling
I finally get through
Feel me love
Reaching out to you
No doubt about it
You are far away
Long distance love
Yesterday and today
Long distance Love
The most challenging kind
A true real love
Is not easy to find
Long distance love
Yesterday and today
Please have no sorrow
We'll make love tomorrow
Long distance love
Long distance love
Come here
Hear what I say
Long distance love
Long distant love
My beautiful
Lovely Ese
Long distance love
Long distance love
My beautiful

Lovely Lady
Long distance love
Long distance love
My sweet
Sweet baby
Long distance love
Long distance love
My sweet
Sweet lady
Long distance love
Yesterday and today
Please have no sorrow
We'll make love tomorrow

Share a Smile

Looking at your eyes
And your beautiful smile
Looking at your eyes
For a long long while
Looking at your smile
And looking at your eyes
Want to kiss those lips
And hold your hips
Looking at you
Hour after hour
Looking at you
My beautiful flower
Your pretty white teeth
And your pretty smile
I want to hold you
A long long while
Holding you
Hour after hour
Lay with you
Feel my power
I really love
Looking in your eyes
Looking at your smile
For a long long while
Dialing your numbers
Hour after hour
To talk with you
And smile for a while
I love looking in
your beautiful eyes awhile

soon we'll kiss and hug
and share a smile
come with me
to our suite
relax your head
and your feet
loving you
hour after hour
loving you
showing you my power

Ese Baby

I love
The color of you eyes
Dreaming of kissing your lips
Admiring your thighs
I love your
Beautiful hips
I love your mind
My treasured one of a kind
I am still dreaming of kissing your lips
Respecting and protecting you
And squeezing you pretty hips
I will see you soon
Loving you with a tune
From midnight
To the next day at noon
I love you
In my heart and mind
Your outer and inner beauty
Are so hard to find
Kissing your breasts
Kissing your lips
Squeezing your hips
Kissing your lips
The time has come
For us to finally unite
You better know
I will love you right
My God Bless
Our love Ese
From his heaven
Above!

Six More Days

Six more days
Our visa time
Is near
My sweetie dear
Six more days
You ESE baby
Are on your way
To share my day
And my night
Living and showing
Loving you right
Learning and growing
Love from
A small seed
Ese my baby
You are what I need
Waiting more than
3 long years
wondering if you baby
would save yourself for me
I can now see
You moving
toward me
my sweetie baby
I sense your presence
I love your essence
The way you think
The way you walk
The way you love
The way you talk

Six more days
We are in this phase
Finding our way
Out of the maze
To find each other
My lady Wife and lover

Our Relationship

We are in
A phase
We are in a
A haze
We are wrapped up
Together on this trip
We are totally involved
In our relationship
Heading toward
Each other
Face to face
Finally together
We are in
This mist
Headed for
Marital bliss
We are projecting
Love together
When we marry
May it be forever!
We are in love
Enclosed in this cloud
We will open the door
Our love will flow
In our motion
with love and devotion
We will make love
with all of our emotion
We will live
And love life

When we are
Husband and wife
We are wrapped up
Together on this trip
We are totally involved
In our relationship
We are in
This mist
Headed toward
Marital bliss!!!!!!!!!!!!!!!

Blessed with your real picture

May we be
Blessed
With blessed happiness
And loving togetherness
May we
be blessed
with love
and happiness
May we
May we embrace
And love each other
My beautiful Grace
Let us live
In unity
You with your
Loveliness
Us together
With happiness
A caress of sweetness
And end our loneliness
I want you
Your real picture
In my life
As my wife
You real picture
You in my life
As my lover,
woman and wife
May we share
Real togetherness

May we share
Love and happiness
In all of
Love's fullness
In all of
Love's wholeness
Love with all
The smoothness
With all
The coolness

You are so Beautiful to me

Written by Ukali for Ese Ohe

Beauty Radiates
From within
Before being lovers
We are best friends
Your picture is in my eye
Longing for you
To solidify our tie
You are so
Beautiful to me
Let's turn you
And I into we
We pray to GOD
To give the world a tap
We'll be together
Just like that
Loving each other
Forever will be our
Priority endeavor
With our solid Foundation
Our love will be our sensation
On day one
Or day two
I am going
To marry you
Let's turn you
And I into we
You are so
Beautiful to me!

Thick and Thin

Ese is my
Best Friend
Loving me through
Thick and Thin

When we
Are apart
Times are
Very Thin

When we
Marry
Very Quickly
Love will be thick

I will marry
You on sight
I love you
And know it's right

Loving you
When it's thick
Loving you
When it's thin

Keep on being
My best friend
When it's thick
or when it's thin

At every station
Focus - I love you
Temptation no
My love will shine through

as I wait for you
and you for me
we love true
through thick and thin

Love me true
Through thick and thin
My Sweet Ese
And my best friend

When I Kiss

When I kiss
Your sweet breast
With a soft touch
I will kiss the best
When I kiss
Your sweet lips
When the lipstick
is on until it's off
Kissing you when
Your clothes are on
Kissing you when
Your clothes are off
When I kiss
Your sweet breast
It will be togetherness
I will kiss with tenderness
When I kiss your lips
It will be nearness
Love and happiness
Love at it's very best
We'll celebrate
Our togetherness
We'll celebrate
Our success
Loving each other
In loneliness
Through the long distance
Praying for our togetherness
So we can share
The same time and space

So I can kiss you all
Over your beautiful face
When I kiss
Your sweet breast
We will have passed
The test
Hold on Ese Ohe
My sweet baby
We'll be together soon
Enjoying each other til noon
We'll celebrate
Our marriage
We'll celebrate
Way above average
We'll be together
Married forever
It will be soon
Enjoying each other till noon
When I kiss
Your sweet breast
Love and happiness
Love at it's very best

Love is deep for you honey

My love is deep
The love we give
Is what we reap
My love is on you
From your head to your feet
For you baby
My love is steep
Feeling love for you
Love I want to keep
My love for you!
My love is deep
Taller than
A mountain peak
Love me true so
So love, we will reap
For you my honey
You are so sweet
My love is on you
May our love remain deep
United together
With the love we reap
Build our love up
Higher than the highest peak
My love for you
Is Sweet and deep
For our minds and hearts
This love we must keep!
Without love, we sink
Love is our link
We will stay together

If we love each other!
I flew across
The ocean deep
To see your face
And so we could meet
Come meet me here
And be my wife
May our love last
As long as we have life

I See Us

I see our silhouettes
Making love together
I see us loving each other
Now and forever
Enjoying peace of mind
Making our love
One of a kind
Two souls
United minds
A marriage binds
Enjoying love: all kinds
One mind
Until our time
I see us getting together
I see our silhouettes
Making love together
I see us
Loving each other

I Want You

From Larry To Ese
I want you
Be my bride
I want you
By my side
So bring it on
Leave your home
Can you feel this poem
Come to our home
I am waiting for you
To land
So I can put
My ring on your hand
And walk with you
For eternity
I love you
and you love me too!
Walk hand in hand
Share the journey
Share honey and lemons
Make a life with me
Sharing our life
Man and Wife
Share love together
Loving you forever!!!

Six More Days

Six more days
Our visa time
Is near
My sweetie dear
Six more days
You ESE baby
Are on your way
To share my day
And my night
Living and showing
Loving you right
Learning and growing
Love from
A small seed
Ese my baby
You are what I need
Waiting more than
3 long years
wondering if you baby
would save yourself for me
I can now see
You moving
toward me
my sweetie baby
I sense
your presence
I love
your essence
The way you think
The way you walk

The way you love
The way you talk
Six more days
We are in this phase
Finding our way
Out of the maze
To find
each other
My lady
Wife and lover

When We

When we are
Between the sheets
When our souls
And hearts meet
You are so
Special to me
I want to
Give you a treat
When we
When we meet
You'll love me
And be so sweet
Sugar won't be
So sweet
And Salt
Won't be salty
Til you are
In my arms
When we sweet
When we meet

Why are

Why are you Black Women
So beautiful
So dutiful
So truthful
Why are Black Women
Why are Black Women?
So beautiful
Because you
are a beautiful
Reflection of us
More spectacular
Than Bling Bling
Our very own
African Queen
Your smile has got the zing
My beautiful Black Queen
My beautiful Black Queen
Wear my ring
Why are Black Women
So beautiful

Love Poem

This is not a poem
But a love song
As the rain falls
I wish I could
Hear your calls
Yet you are
Too far away
To hear me
Reach out to you today!
Then comes the night
Delta thunder and light
This is not a song
This is a love poem
Feel you coming on
Very soon you'll be home
And I will see your face
Here in this place
So far away
Wish you were here
Wish you were here
Closer to me my dear
Remember this is no song
This is a love poem
Wishing you were here
Closer my sweetie dear!
A long distance love affair
Is a love so deep to share
Closer my sweetie dear
Wish you were hear

Woman of My Dreams
Dialog with a black Woman Part 4

You are
The woman of my dreams
You are a queen among queens
And the most beautiful thing
I want to give you my ring
You are the girl of my dreams
I want to make
You my queen
I can talk to you
On the phone
But I want you
In my home
Sweet Woman
In my dreams,
I want to bust the seam
So I can become your King
So you can be my queen
So you can emerge
From my dreams
And be my real Queen.

Soon we

Soon we
Will be together
Hooking up
Marrying you forever

Soon we
Will touch each other
Fall deeper in love
In bed undercover

Soon we
Will be one
Soon please
May the day soon come

Soon we
Will marry
Soon we
You and me

Soon we
Thinking of no other
Soon we
Loving forever

Love Me True

Love me true
And I'll
Never be
Through with you
From the first
Day I see you
The first time
I kiss your face
I'll pay attention
And love you too
I'll never be
Through with you
I promise
To hold you tight
I will always
Treat you right
I will love
Getting to know you
Looking in your eyes
and close, close ties
Sharing my world
Respecting your
point of view
really getting to know you
Love me true
And I'll
Never be through with you

Pretty African Lips

I want to kiss you
But I can't
I want to touch you
A reality it may seam
But that's only a dream
A whole continent away
Wished I could touch you
The first thing this day
Yet you are far way
I want to kiss your lips
I wonder about you
From your laps, thighs and hips
I really want to kiss
Your pretty lips
So I'm writing this poetry
Stirred up by your picture
Thinking of your pretty lips
Wondering about your pretty hips

Loving You All Seasons

We will do
Our thing
I will love you
Throughout the spring
I will love you
Throughout the summer
Like a long distance runner
When it is hot
Love is the tool
I am no fool
Love is the rule
I will make you cool
I will love you
I won't stop
When it's cool
Or when it is hot
I will hear your call
Don't worry at all
I'll love you
In the fall
We will see winter
Rain, chilly and cold
I will keep you warm
Through rain and storm
For all times
For heartfelt reasons
I will love you
All seasons

My Beautiful Wife

I want to
See eye to eye
With you
I want to see
What you see
I want you
To see what I see
Eye to eye
Nose to nose
Lips to lips
Love to love
I want to see
You yesterday
Today
And tomorrow
Like a bright sunny day
I want you to
Come my way
My African queen
Brand new thing
My beautiful new wife
For the rest of my life

Written 10/24/03 10:30pm

Get through

I tried to call
You are not here
If your were here
This is what
I would say dear
I love talking to you
Longing for us to be near
In love
But distance I fear
What I really want
Is to bring you near
My beautiful dear
Can you hear?
Tried to call
But I couldn't get through,
This is what I would
Say to you

God Will Make a Way

Go will make a way
I will unite with a wife
soon one day
and we'll be on our way

Don't rush
the land is lush
open the door
of a blessing in store

She will be nice
and very sweet
she will be
the real deal

Soul sister Black Queen
And I'll be
her Black king
And the day will come
we'll unite as one
We'll live together
live life and have fun

Thoughts of You Dreams of You

Speaking with you
Thoughts of
Touching you too
Passion dripping
Like sweat
Passion dripping
Like it is wet
Dreaming of
Marrying you
Spending days together
And nights too
Precious thoughts
Of meeting eye to eye
We'll hold each other
As days and nights go by
Seeing you
If only in my mind
Planning scheming
Your love I must find
Dreams of you
Beautiful thoughts too
Of the time real soon
When I will touch you
And you will
Touch me
We will be wrapped up
And touchi feeli
I will know you
And you will know me
I embrace you Grace

Ese you and I, we
Never forget
The chase
Never forget
I love you Grace
Thoughts of you
Holding you too
Squeezing you tight
Ese me and you

4-year courtship

As I look
At your pretty eyes
And feel my
temperature rise
I realize
it's only
a picture yet
do I fantasize?
From a 4 year courtship
To our marriage
Developing
our relationship
Looking in
Your pretty eyes
No surprise
You are the prize
This is where
We begin
Will you be
My best friend
Stay with me
I'll hold you tightly
Let our love
Never ever end
Visa is approved
We will soon marry
And hit a groove
With a love that is smooth
Whip up a love
That is ever

So smooth
In your groove
Cause the time
Has finally come
Two will melt
Into one
Moving closer
And closer
Until we are married
and living together
You are
smart and clever
I will love you
forever

A Million Times

I kissed your picture
A million times
And read you love rhythms
Through telephone lines
I prayed for
This day to come
When our two souls
Will merge as one
We waited
Not patiently
You are so pretty
Inside and out, so lovely
Now is the time
Please be my wife
Come and love me
And share my life
Our time is near
Sweet Ese my dear
We will marry
And celebrate with cheer
I kissed your picture
A million times
And read you love rhythms
Through telephone lines
And the intensity
Of your stare
You could see my soul
My love, I know you care
When I meet you
Face to face

Eye to eye
Oh my, oh my!!
Time I could
never find
To get you
Out of my mind
You know I love you
And your sweet voice
Let's get married
You are my choice
I kissed your picture
A million times
And read you love rhythms
Through telephone lines

All These Years

All of these years
Calling you on the phone
Make you my wife
Of my very own
All these years
Sending folders of email
All my dreams
On a grand scale
All these years
Waiting to marry you
All of these years
Wanting to marry you
Cold nights alone
Your voice warmed
Me up on the phone
Bring my smile back on
Your sweet letters
cuts right through my heart
to my soul
when you come on bold
All these years
With love and fears
I want to touch you dear
Sometime this year
Three long years
Calling you on the phone
All these years
Waiting to marry you
And know we know
We'll marry

For sure
And you will be my honey
After all these years
You'll be in my arms
We'll share our love
arms and charms
Preparing for you
Loving you too
After three years
I'm going to marry you

From This Dream

The cloud covered
The sun
And the moon
Til noon
Your jet
Landed
And I was
no longer stranded
The cloud
disappeared
The sun
Reappeared
As the sun
Shined through
I found myself
Embraced by you
My Ese
My beautiful queen
Then I woke up
From this dream
Still waiting for you
And yet
Time is closer too
My lovely lady
Our time is near
Very soon you
will be here
In my
loving arms
and love

filled charms
My Ese
My Beautiful queen
Only you can
Make real, this dream

Life Long Hug

My love for you is
Deeper than a river
I want to be
Your caregiver
To you I want
To deliver
Love longer
than a river
I want you here
Sweetie dear
Please prepare
to come near
I will lie down awhile
And wake up to your smile
It will be so nice
We will live in paradise
I want another
Hug from you
A life long hug
To keep us true
As you know
Only you will do
And you must know
How much I love you
Come and feel my empty nest
And relieve my stress
Get here quick
We must try our very best

Married to you
Living with you
Enjoying our life
as husband and wife.

My Queen

You are
My love
You are
My Queen
When we marry
We'll have everything
When I am you king
And you are my queen
I called you
Today on your cell phone
I'll come get you
If the wait goes on
When we spoke
With your pretty voice
No doubt in my voice
You are my choice
Until that day come
Realize you are the one
We know what it is: True,
That we are going through
Ese you have
My heart
Grace you are
My queen
When we marry
We'll have everything
When I am your King
And you are my Queen

Now and Forever

Let us come together
Now and forever
Love each other
Come my love
Accomplish our dream
If we have love
We have everything
Come with your
beauty and steam
We will make
A great team
Commit our love
To each other
To live together
Now and forever
We will be happy
We will be together
Holding you my lover
Now and forever
I salute you
Ese my wife to be
You and I together
Now and Forever

Real Love

Real love
Can grow
Individually and
Collectively
Until there is
A love overflow
And we all know
As the love will grow
And consolidate
A love that is great
With give and take
This is the love
I want to make
Real Love will grow
Our hearts will glow
like a volcanic eruption
Our love will flow
Real love will then grow
as our hearts are aglow
And our love will flow
Real love
With give and take
This is the love
I want to make

Send um Catch um

Will you
catch um for me
If I send um
To you
Will you
Catch um catch um
And hold um hold um
For me
Will you
hold um hold um
tightly too
If I send um to you
Will you hold um hold um
If I
Send um send um
Hold me so tightly
Will you
Hold um
hold um
And hold me so tightly
We'll be making
love sincerely
Husband and wife
And lovers for life
I go send um
With all my love
Catch um liker a glove
with all my love
So please
don't forget

hold um hold um
and hold me so tightly
I go send um
Send um to you
Please hold um hold um
And hold me so tightly
Catch all my love
Bless our love from above
Catch um like a glove
Holds um hold um my love

The Chase

This is the chase
Of all chases
To unite our spaces
Love is the basis
This is the chase
of all chases
our love
is the basis
Take me to
Your special places
Take me to your
Special places
Chasing you
in many places
Filing applications
And cases
Cause love love love
is the basis
Begging people
of all races
This is the chase
Of all chases
Hearing no from
So many faces
Filing notices
Love is the basis
This is the chase
Of all chases

Take me to
your special spaces
Take me to your
Special places

The Longest Night

The longest
Night of the year
I want you
Right here
And make our place
A love nest Grace
So I can see
Your smiling face
Turn the heat up
My sweet buttercup
Bring your passion
Feel my love in action
Feel my emotion
Your love is my potion
I am loving you
with my love in motion
Our love will
heat and steam
my sweet love
My sweet queen
The longest night
Of this year
You are there
I wished you were here
I hope
you know
How I feel
Ese my lady, I am real
Our time is
almost here

My sweet
Ese dear
Ese baby
Sweetie dear
Long distant love
You'll soon be here

Before June

I love you Ese
From deep within
That is because
You're my best friend
My mate I can relate to
Deep in my heart
Lay my love true
For sweet Ese—you
I look forward
To the day
Not too
Far away
When we will
Share an embrace
And you'll
Be in my arms Grace
The first day
I Saw your face
I fell deeper
In love with you Grace
So wait
for me
While I
wait for you
Our day will be here soon
We'll share a hug and a tune
I'll surely
See you by June

So Much More

We can give
Each other the pleasure
And treat each
Like valuable treasure
Be that virtuous woman
And I'll be your great man
And together we can
Walk through life
Hand in hand
You can be my wife
We can be lovers and friends
As long as we are
the ones that win
We can open that door
And have so much more
WE can make our life
Just like paradise.

Dedicated to Ese Ohe Mamodu.

Ese in Cali, No Marriage Today

It was a Thursday and I am going to work my norm as a high school administrator. No, I will pick up my friend Easter, in Hayward and drive to San Francisco International Airport.

After four years of on the phone and email communications and my October 5th visit to Nigeria, to meet my fiancée, I was going to the Airport to pick her up.

We picked up my friend's niece and my fiancée and took them back to her uncle's spot by previous arrangement. Ese and I had signed an affidavit to marry each other within 90 days of her arrival as part of the fiancée visa process. Ese and I also promised each other that we would marry each other on day 1 or day 2 of her arrival in the USA.

As soon as Ese had enjoyed a meal prepared by her uncle and relaxed a while, I began speaking with Ese and when I was comfortable and speaking with Ese one on one, I bent down on one knee and asked Ese to marry me.

I brought out my wedding band to show I was serious. Ese said yes, but not today, we can marry tomorrow. Then we tried the ring and it fit her perfectly. She smiled. Anyone would have thought that this was a good sign. By this time Easter arrived and said this is a good sign.

I noticed Ese being very sleepy so I left, but not before embracing Ese, but she turned away her face! I thought it was shyness. I left while Ese was preparing to sleep saying I will be here tomorrow so we can go to breakfast and then go to marry in Oakland at the Alameda County Court, as we had discussed the matter.

I arrived on Friday dressed in a suit ready to get married to Ese. When I arrived she was still in her Lagos pajamas. Her mood was withdrawn. Finally, after her uncle asked if she was ready or going to get ready there was a stand off. Ese finally came to me and said her Dad said she could not marry me today.

There is a stand off that lasts for hours. We speak but Ese is in a distant cold mood. I still have my ring in my pocket.

I strongly urge Ese to act as an adult and marry me. I tell that eventually everything will work out.

I try to be reassuring. Ese remains headstrong. Easter explains how we have both taken off our jobs so that we, Ese and I, can make the next step. But several hours of patiently working through promises to marry, my wish to be her husband and take care of her, she never dresses and said she is sleepy and jet lagged.

I leave and sadly driving back to Antioch instead of going to the Madison St. Alameda County House to marry Ese and take my bride home!

About 5:30 to 6:30 pm, I receive a call from my friend Easter and he said his brother left the decision to Ese. He said I should come back to Hayward and get Ese and spend the weekend getting to know her better so we can see if we really want each other.

I arrived at 7:30pm, Ese has been crying, there is tension. So naturally, I sought to comfort Ese while realizing Easter is really giving us a chance to sort it all out!

I wondered how did we get to this point with all of Ese's promises to be a great lover, wife, and mother—made repeatedly when I called her on her cell phone in Nigeria.

Ese and I loaded up two overnight bags into my car. I was happy but she was sad. I kept asking her about her promises to be my wife,; she kept repeating her dad's opposition. I asked how does she feel. Ese face was sad so I asked Ese what would make you happy? She said, "Take me to the mall."

I took her to the Southland Mall Macy's, some boutiques and finally Mervyns. As we passed the Victoria Secret outlet, I offered to go in there but she stubbornly refused.

I ran into Murphy Matier—an elementary, middle school, and high school classmate—and introduced Murphy to Ese. Ese was standoffish. Murphy and I wrapped up our conversation and I again offered to take Ese into the Victoria's Secret store again she refused.

In Macy's, Ese picked out two pair of shoes and some socks. In Mervyns's, Ese picked out two low riser jeans. I paid for the jeans and said we should head for Antioch. Ese's new items gave her a temporary smile but when I said I am heading for Antioch, she said no she wants to return to her Uncle's place. I convinced Ese as a compromise to go to a hotel in Castro Valley this was a nice place.

I signed her in and as soon as we got everything in her room she insisted that I go to Antioch and pick her up in the morning. She assured me after a good night's sleep in the hotel she would be herself and we could get to know each other better. I took her at her word!

I told Ese I could not go to Antioch but that I could sleep in the room and not try anything. She again insisted I leave so she could sleep.

The walk out of that room and back to the lobby was one of the longest and loneliest and most embarrassing walks ever past the male clerk who had just rented the room to us. I could not sleep in the car so I walked back to the room at 6 am and found Ese fully dressed at the door.

Looking back on it she may have been trying to ditch me then but maybe she was really coming to check on me as she said.

If You Knew
After midnight Poetry

If you knew how much
I want to kiss your lips sweetie
Would you run away?
Or run to me

If you knew
What would you do?
If I was hugging you
And you were hugging me too

If you really knew
What would you say?
Would you marry me right away?
This very day?

If you actually knew
And felt the same way
Would you give our love
A beautiful start today

If you knew how
I want to kiss you
Tell me, Tell me
What would you do?

If you know
Like I know I love you
Tell me Tell me
What would you do?

If we made love
With you on top
Would we make love?
Til your love drop

As my wife
And best friend
Would we then
Do it again

And if I
Got you really hot
Would you love me?
And never stop

And again and again
When you want it
Love you good
Until you drop it

If you really knew
How much I love you?
Would you marry me today?
Or would you run away?

Sunday and Ese's New Strategy

I didn't sleep well in the car but I slept in the car for Ese so she would feel comfortable.

However, when I entered the room at 7:43 or so we kind of lazed around, talked about matters and every time I looked in her eye to find the spark of something, I did not find it.

Suddenly, Ese said I am moving in with you so take me back to my uncle's place so I can get all of my things. Was she for real or was she just saying what I wanted to hear? I thought to myself, Ese was finally coming around! We worked together and then there was even a hug that was ever so short.

We left the hotel and headed back to my friend's place. Once we got there my friend was happy to see us and when Ese said she was there to move all of her things into my place we were surprised but happy.

The three of us moved her things into my car but not before Ese asked me to take some pictures of her near her uncle's place. It was Saturday so this time we started to Antioch by 580 to 13 to 24 to 68N to 242 and up Highway 4 to Antioch.

Once there Ese and I had several long talks. I explained many reasons why I loved her and wanted to marry her. I took a shower and cooked some food. Then I welcomed my sister Ann and continued cooking while Ese and Ann spoke like two accountants—both have a BA in accounting.

I finished cooking and served the food. Then opened a bottle of wine, poured libation outside on my balcony to the ground below and then prayed over the food. We enjoyed our dinner. Soon Ann left.

I then explained the way forward after we get married constantly looking for the sparkle in her eyes, that I never found. After all of the details, I then asked if I could bring the rest of her things in Ese said no that she cannot sleep here in my place and would I take her to a hotel again.

After a long discussion, I decided to do as she requested and took her to a hotel in this area. I checked her in as she affirmed over and over again that she would be ready to meet my family and carry on after one more good night's sleep in the hotel. I was tired as I could be and could no longer refuse the strong urge to sleep. I checked Ese in, left her in the hotel with one of my cell phones, my ring on her finger and this manuscript. I kissed her on her cheek still looking for a little tenderness and warmth but finding very little.

Ese asked me to meet her for breakfast at 10 am. I drove back to my place and slept like a baby. I was up at 7 am and I was knocking on Ese's hotel room door by 9 am. After knocking at her door for en minutes, I returned to the motel office.

Since I rented the room, I asked for a duplicate room key. The hotel clerk gave me another plastic key but said I could leave the card in the room. As I walked away there was a loud laugh from the clerk.

I thought nothing of the clerk's laugh until I got up to Ese's room, opened the door and found the room completely empty. At this moment my cell phone rang there was a message. I listened to the message and called my other cell phone and Ese answered. I asked what was really going on and Ese said she was going to get herself together. Then she warned me that the battery was getting weak. Suddenly the phone went dead.

Heart in Pain

Hurting soul and body
And my mind
For love
For love of one of a kind
Looking for
Your love
Preparing
Praying to GOD above
Then you showed
Very cold
Pain for my soul
And full
Of deceit
Pain like rain
Pain is my stain
So this is
Your Passion
For me your love
Is fiction?
Heart in pain
Pain like rain
A deceived love
Is a shame!

My Queen

A four-year
Courtship
Correspondence
Communicating
Relationship
We met
Together at
SFO to
Pick up my fiancé
So you deceived me
So cleverly
Instead of
Leveling with me
Took my love on
Left me all alone
Took my ring
Leaving a painful sting
Your move
Was very clever
Our loss
We're not together
Tak ing a licking
Keep on ticking
We could have had everything
Fooled by my queen

Took Your Love Away

Why did you
Take love away
Did I listen
To what you had to say

How could you?
Love that way
No Love today
You left yesterday

Arrived in
Broad light
You ran in
The night

Took your love
Away one night
Before we could
Hold each other tight

Is this your love?
Or was I too blind to see
In your soul
Was there love for me?

I know the answer
I knew from the day
You took my ring
And took your love away

From This Dream

The cloud covered
The sun
And the moon
Til noon
Your jet
Landed
And I was
No longer stranded
The cloud
Disappeared
The sun
Reappeared
As the sun
Shined through
I found myself
Embraced by you
My Ese
My beautiful queen
Then I woke up
From this dream
Still waiting for you
And yet
Time is closer too
My lovely lady
Our time is near
Very soon you
Will be here

In my
Loving arms
And love
Filled charms
My Ese
My Beautiful queen
Only you can
Make real, this dream

Flopping Whopping

I want your
Flopping whooping
I have love
Waiting for you
You got love too
You and I
very soon
We'll sing
A together tune
Our sun
Will shine
We'll make
A beautiful rhyme
Going deeper
And deeper
Getting sweeter
And sweeter
Til you are numb
Til you come
We are two
Who become one
Smacking good
Like loving should
I would touch you
If I could
I want your
Floopin Whoppin
When we dance
We'll be hoppin
Loving you

Never stoppin
Floppin whoppin
Whoppin Floppin
I want you
Here and now
Got to have you
Some how
Loving you
Never Stoppin
I want your
Whopping Hopping
Take you dancing
Take you shopping
Loving you
Never stopping
Get your visa
In a few days
Come here
Enjoy my loving Ways
Share my life
With you as my wife
We can build
A love so true
Loving you
Never stoppin
I want your
Floppin hoppin
I want you
Floopin Whoppin
Loving you
Never stoppin

Head to Your Toes

From the tip of your toes
All up and down
I will love you
In my town

I will love you
With sensitivity
I will hold you
So soft and tenderly

Poetically
Patiently
Joyfully and
Lovingly

Love me
So I can
Love you so much
With my mind and touch

Settle with me
So we can become we
And hold each other
As my wife and lover

Come here baby
Come here my lady
Make sure you are ready
Make sure you are steady

So I can
Love you totally
My queen, your king
With love we have everything

I will always
Take it slow
I want you
To know I know!

Come to me
My pretty rose
I'll love you
From you head to your toes

Love you
From your head
To the tips of
Your pretty toes

Fighting For You

We'll climb
The hills
Work together
And develop new skills

Fighting for you
Loving you too
Fighting for you
Doing what I got to do

Calling you and
Waking you up
Calling people is my sequel

Writing email
Sending you good vibes
So we can unite
And share our lives

Enjoying plush valleys
Climbing the hills
Like a team working together
Enjoying our love's thrills

Working together
For our progress
Making love
The very best

Climbing and enjoying
Loving and growing
Living and loving in unity
We will be a family

We'll climb
the hills
work together
Developing new skills

Smooth and Slow, Private Poem for Ese

Hearing your
Voice today
Set me off
In a special way

And the sweet
words said
Keeping
Our love fed

Through our
last separation
before marriage
and unification

May the days
Go by
Til again we meet
And marry Ese lovely

Smooth and slow
Light as a feather
Smooth and slow
So you will glow

I love
Your laugh that way
And what you
Said today

Fun in London
Or Lagos

Or Antioch
Near San Francisco

Very soon
Months past June
We'll make love
From night til noon

In just
a little time
You in my arms—
everything fine

May the days
go quick
So we can
Get to it

Smooth and slow
Hear my flow
Love you more
You will glow

Light as a feather
Smooth and slow
We ll be together
You will glow

Smooth and slow
Are you ready?
Smooth and slow
I'll go with your flow

Smooth and slow
You open the door
Smooth and slow
When you are ready to go

When Love Flows

When love flows
Both ways
Love grows
And brightens days
As we enter
The love phase
Realize real love is hard to
Find these days
It is our choice
To enter the love phase
Let our love
Flow both ways
May we enjoy
Better days
Sharing love
In our love phase
With love that flows
Both ways!

September 1, 2007 Update

We continue our correspondence and make plans to meet in London now that we have exhausted the first US Visa. Here is the letter that led to the final clarification!

Dear Sir/Madam: Good Morning,

CC Lagos Consulate Chief, Visa Section

My name is Larry Ukali Johnson-Redd and I am writing you regarding my fiancée Ese Ohe Grace Momodu.

We have been involved with each other 4 and 1/2 years and we have always planned to get married since 2003. However upon her arrival there was an unexpected series of events that occurred when we were finally in the same place—April 20, 2007 Ese arrived in the USA. We never said we would not marry each other; however, there were areas we needed to smooth out with her family that prevented us from marrying when Ese was here and Ese returned to Nigeria in June 2, 2007.

Since Ese returned to Nigeria to quit her job and return to me for marriage, she has sought an appointment unsuccessfully or had job and flooding (rainy season) problems arriving at the US Consulate-Lagos on time for her appointments one or two times. She has requested an appointment several times since then most recently July 13, 2007. Ese has not received a new appointment despite her new requests. So I am requesting that Ese's visa status be clarified since Ese was told by a US Consulate staff person she needs a new visa on July 13, 2007 when she last visited the consulate on Victoria Island!. And if she has permission that it be made plain and put in writing as soon as possible!

At the door of the US Consulate Ese was told to wait for an email notification of an appointment; however, to date Ese has not received that email. Ese will certainly make any appointment you make for her to the best of her abilities!

Meanwhile I have been calling Karen Tedford, Ellen Tausha US House of Representatives honorable member that I vote for regularly. Karen Tedford has communicated with you the Chief of the VISA Section about our visa request for years and shared my disappointment when things did not work out. Karen Tedford also understands I want Ese and I to have another chance to join me and Ese has assured me she is ready to leave Nigeria within 2 weeks of receiving a written notice that she can proceed to the USA—so she can quit her job in a professional manner.

This morning when I spoke to Karen she said that all Ese needed to do according to you was buy a ticket and fly here to California. If and when Ese is allowed to leave Nigeria, she will arrive in my loving arms. Karen said Ese did not need to go to the Consulate again. However, there is a is the designation of 1 entry on Ese's visa and unless she has a document from the US Consulate that says 2 entries or 1 more entry she would be scared to quit her job and travel because Immigration agents might not have the same understanding.

I believe what Karen Tedford said is true but I need you to call Ese in to the Lagos Consulate and properly update her visa—the part that says 1 entry and make it 2 entries or multiple entry so she can travel here confident that she will not encounter problems. Time is passing so a quick response will be totally appreciated by Ese and I.

1. You could reply Ese and me directly by responding directly to this email.
2. You can call Ese at _____ and invite Ese in for an interview.
3. You can give me an answer to my question about 2 entries or multiple entries right away and advise me on how to proceed.

Please respond quickly for me so I may capture my true love Ese Ohe Grace Momodu's heart and marry Ese in California before her visa time period runs out in September 2007. I want Ese, my fiancée here as soon as possible. This is a desperate plea of a Black Man in America in love with Ese Ohe Grace Momodu.

Please help me right away!!!

Sincerely,

Larry Ukali Johnson-Redd

See You Soon

Sitting under
A full moon
Hoping to
See you soon

You are
A sweet tune
And I'm hoping
To see you soon

The moon shines
so bright
But not as
Bright as you

I
Love you
Do you love?
Me too

Hoping to
See you soon
I am hoping
You share my tune

Hoping to see you
Very soon
So we can
Share a room

Hoping we'll
Be together
And know each other
Much better

So I sing
this tune
Dreaming of
Loving till noon

Sitting under
A full moon
We'll share life
London and a room

Love and respect
In my tune
Hoping to
See you soon

I will marry you
In London
Hoping to
See you soon

Standing under
A full moon
Love and happiness
See you soon

My African Dream

You are
my African dream
You are
My African Queen

You I await
You are my Fate

Today you are there
I am here
Let's meet up
Somewhere

You are my
Wife—
To—Be,
Sweetie

As my wife
Feel my charms
Enjoying my love
In my arms

Strong like Nzinga
The African Queen
You are my
Nigerian Queen

You are
my African Dream
You are
My African Queen

And the Love and Happiness

Is anything as smooth
As a man's smoothness
When a brother shares
A Black Woman's happiness

When we are blessed
When we pass the test
When love was missed
Not as we wished

Yet happiness
Is right on target
May we get together?
And never forget

I want you
To know I know
How I want
You to glow

But you should know
That I know
For love to flow
You got to take it slow

And we shall
Plan our run
And have fun
in London

Dreaming wondering
Not sitting on the fence
Merging with you
Is common sense

Yet long
is the wait
My love is an earthquake
It is you I want to shake

I'm waiting with
The coolness and smoothness
for the passion and heat, your smile
And the love and happiness

My Bling Bling

You will
Enrich my life
When we marry
And you become my wife

Your love will
Make my life rich
Come my way
This very day

Come here
My sweet dear
From home land hemisphere
Sweet dear come near

Enter a world
with me
So we
can be we

In our home of love
Our sweet relationship
In our marriage
Merge 2 into 1 ship

Share a real love
Share our life
With me as your husband
And you as my wife

Let your voice
Bring my life joy
A joy we can share
I'll show you I care

So we can share
Our life our smile
And talk for
A long long while

Cause my life
With out you
Is incomplete
I need you my sweet

My lovely Black Queen
You are my Bling Bling
My sweeties come to me
So we can be we

My sweet lovely beautiful lady
Come and be my sweet Baby
My lovely African Queen
You are my Bling Bling

A Happy Birthday Poem
For Ese Ohe Grace Momodu my Queen and My Bling Bling
Emailed to Ese Dec.1, 2007

I Made Love

I made love to you
In my dream
I made love to you
Ese my lovely Queen

I want to hold
You in reality
I want to kiss you
When you're so close to me

I made love to you
Kissing you in my dream
Come to my reality
And make sweet love to me

I don't want this dream
Anymore my sweetie
I want you in my arms
In my reality

But I will keep
You lovely in my dream
While I await you in reality
As my lovely queen

I WILL KISS YOU
if only in my dream
Until the day you arrive
As my lovely queen

I made love to you
Kissing you in my dream
Come to my reality
And make sweet love to me

So I can share
My reality and life
So I can be your husband
And you can be my wife

Are You

Are you coming here
To fall deeper in love
And deeper in love
So we can be we

Are you bringing passion?
To make a true love connection
So we can have friction
In a loving direction

So we can seal
Our love in marriage
So we can feel
Martial love that is for real

So I can
receive you
with open arms
And love filled charms

I want your love
I'm lonely for you
I want you to
Love me too, yes I do

I'll pick you up
At the airport
With a love filled kiss
and hug you just like this

This is my take
Only real love
Will I make
How long must I wait?

I want you
To feel comfortable
I will love you right
I know I am able

Till then I dream
Of marrying you my queen
You are my Bling Bling
Please Ese wear my ring

ARE YOU COMING
To fall deeper
And deeper in love
So we can be we

So We Can Be We

Come to me
My sweetie
Love each other
So we can be we

Love me and
Hug and kiss me too
So we can be we
Me and you

So we can be we
Fly from your country
So we can be we
Ese so lovely and pretty

Fly to me
Ese my sweetie
For you and me
So we can be we

Dreaming about you
So much
I can't sleep
Thinking of you my sweet

Dreaming about
You
Visualizing you
In my sight

So we
Can be we
So we
Can be we

Your sweet heart
Your sweet mind
Bring your love
So we can be we

Loving you
in my dreams
Seeing you
As my Queen

I always have
You on my mind
Please be lovely
To me sweet and kind

Come into my heart
For a love
That will never
Never ever part

Dreaming of you
Dreaming you and me 2
So we can be we
So we can be we

When Next We Meet

When next we meet
Will you baby be sweet?
I hope to see you soon
When next we meet

Give your self to me
We have been
Communicating
Real love not faking

My love for you
Is live and breathing
Real love not teasing
Real love and pleasing

I'll accept
You humbly
I'll give myself
To you

And love you
Totally
Our love
Will have beauty

And durability
I ask you my sweet
So honorably
Please give yourself to me

My sweet and lovely
Together we will be
In wedded bliss
Eternally

So give your
Self to me
So we
Can be we

Come to me
Not to tease
But to please
With that right tight squeeze

Come to me
Not to tease
Bring me your squeeze
I want you to please

Come to me
Sail the seas
Show me I am yours
We'll open loves doors

Come to me
No need to tease

Love me more and more
Like you mean to please
Wholeheartedly
So we can be we

Our love will sing
When I give you my ring
Please give yourself to me
So we can be we

I'll love you eternally
For a love filled with beauty
My lovely sweetie
So you can love dearie

When next we meet
Please make it sweet
For sweetie to love dearie
When next we meet

Clarification Email

Sunday, March 23, 2008 was a gigantic milestone culminating five years of our long distance relationship. Yet in the most profound dimensions we were no closer than we were when we began. I needed to clarify and sort out our relationship I felt now more than ever. Unless Ese sent me a signed 325 A form we were dead in the water. When Ese mailed the form the last time we were successful in attaining her visa. However, she arrived in a state of confusion and she ran away like a thief in the night!

Maybe I should have washed my hands of Ese at that point. However, Ese called me upon her arrival back to her father's house in Nigeria and insisted we should try for another visa where she would be that real Black Queen for me her Black King! That might have been the best point of departure but I was caught up you know in love irrational and determined to be successful in winning Ese's heart! Somewhere in the scenario of Ese.s life she married someone else!

Here is my Clarification Email:

Hello Ese,

I can no longer take it whatever this is that is happening in your life. First of all every meaningful attempt I have made to communicate with you from my heart has ended without your heartfelt reply. Especially the letter I sent you by DHL and several detailed letters I sent you by email. I do not get the detailed reply I want from you.

Maybe you are too busy pursuing your current career to focus on me. I truly hope that this is not the case but the sudden travel and failure to communicate your innermost feelings about you and me despite my many attempts to reach inside through poetry and conversations where I try but get only one-word answers. It leaves me in a difficult situation on this day; five years after your Uncle Easter and your dad introduced us to each other over the phone!

I really wished you had tried and would try to communicate better your innermost feelings but you haven't, making me wonder if you share with me my most inner feelings of wanting to marry you!

The last detailed letter I emailed you was one seeking clarification. This letter too you did not answer to this very day. Much as I love you and noting the complete lack of email or phone contact over the last 2 and 1/2 weeks, I am lost as to how to explain your actions on certain matters necessary for us to move forward like the return of the 325 Form and your decision not to answer critical questions. I have repeatedly asked you to answer. I really wanted with all my heart the chance to see we become we and marry!

So I am giving you three months to mail the 325 Form to me in my hands here in California. Do I want you? Yes I do! The question in all of this letter is do you want me and if so what are you going to do?

I am preparing to go New York and thought you would be here to accompany me to New York City. Are you undecided about completing the 325 Form?

Oh how that question is on my mind right now and oh how I wish you would give me the definitive answer I seek from you from your heart. So let us agree to resolve these matters of our heart and join together in three months or at least sign and send the form to me if you want us to continue like I want us to continue. But I want a reply from this email as soon as possible from you—from your heart!

Sincerely,
Ukali

Ese 's letter of response answered some of my questions and was the beginning of the end. However. I was still deeply in love and without the rational foundation to understand. All was lost even at this response. Ese termed my attempt at clarification aggressive. But her reply also had some aggression. I felt I had once again opened my heart to Ese so she could rush on in!

Here is Ese's response:

> Hello Larry,
>
> I understand everything you have written and i know how you feel, i can't write a comprehensive email to you right now because am still busy as you said with my career but hopefully i should be thru with everything by next week and i will be back in Lagos
>
> Then we can talk better and really share what we feel for each other, but you sound very aggressive and i don't think that is nice because you already have a career for your self, why don't you want to support me in also building my own career too.
>
> And talking about New York are you relocating to New York? Or just on holiday?
>
> If it is for the just the holiday, i will love to be there with you, but . . . Any way i will call or email you as soon as i get back to Lagos.
>
> yours
> Ese

Here is my response and you can tell I still had my love blinders on! Hello my sweetie Ese,

> I am so happy to hear from you finally. I was in some despair yesterday because I could not even speak to you and yesterday was five years of our meeting and beginning on the path we had both felt would lead to our marriage!

Please my sweetie Ese please try to understand I had not heard from you for over a week. I truly love you and my emotional not aggressiveness was only meant to show how much I miss you and want you in my life now! I am lonely living here in this place all by myself and my prayer to God and my appeal to you is to marry you and be the best husband I could possibly be to you!

I totally support you and your quest for a career of your choice and I remember saying learn all you can. This training came up suddenly and until now you never told me when the training was ending. So please forgive me for wanting you all to my self right away but after five years, and two sort of missed opportunities especially in April when we sat on our long sofa together! I wanted so much to make you comfortable and you my sweetie were uneasy (laugh).

I am going to New York as a chance to perform at the City University of New York and attend a Black Writer's Conference. I will be there in New York for four days! As I fly I will be wishing you were sitting next to me. Maybe I would feel better if I had met you in London or if you stayed longer with me in Antioch (Smile).

However our road to each other has not been as easy as I hope we both would have preferred! Ese I love you so much that I want to marry you and my life will not be complete without you in my life as my wife.

I am yours,
Ukali

Saying Goodbye

Today is Sunday, April 13, 2008. I am sitting in a brake repair shop getting my brakes repaired! Yesterday, Saturday, my first cousin Sam got married. I was there with my mom and many family members from the many different families of our extended family! There Reeds, Garrets, and many others besides us Redds!

Yesterday Saturday April 12, 2008 at 9 am I called Ese. She had returned to Lagos and as usual she was at work or so she told me. I asked if she could speak to me in frank terms and she said yes! I was surprised and shocked but she continued.

So I asked if she could speak to me from the inner most part of her heart and she said okay!

I made it easy by asking Ese if she was going to send the 325 A INS form so we could pursue another fiancée visa. Ese's reply was no! After a deep breath Ese said she wants to complete a master's degree in Nigeria and somehow help to improve Nigeria!

I struggled to keep control of my emotions and I could feel the pain in my heart as the disappointment began to set in!

I began to see why her love always seemed wishy washy, off and on hot and cold really now unreal!

Still I wished her well and she wished me well finally saying stay in touch with your friend Ese! Our conversation was now like our relationship was in free fall and I had no parachute as I fell lower and lower comforted only by the answer to my prayers to God for clarification and resolution that was finally here!

Every now and then Ese and I said goodbye to each other and a lower and lower pitch until I finally dropped the phone hanging up ending our five-year long relationship!

It was a beautiful California day at 85 degrees!

I tried to gather my wits and got ready to attend Sam's wedding with a sad backdrop I wanted desperately to hide!

I felt relieved and hurt, disappointed and determined! Even then in my feelings of despair and disillusionment—I desperately tried to remain positive!

Even though I was hurting, I had a wedding to attend! I thought about how I would heal and live and maybe someday love again but not like this one, my long distance love!

You Can't Lose What You Never Had

You can't lose
What you never had
Maybe if she was with me
I would be so happy
I'll be happy not sad
You can't lose
What you never had

There are some ladies
Faking love is a fad
But a brother feel the pain a tad
She said she loved me
Maybe she lied
No doubt I loved her
But she ditched the ride

I am hurt but not sad
You can't miss
What you never had
Fake love is
A rad fad
You can't miss a love
You never had

Larry Ukali Johnson-Redd, born 1952 in San Francisco, graduated from Balboa High School in 1970 and attended the University in San Francisco where he received a Masters in Public Administration 1976 (MPA).

During his early University days he met Chinwe, a Nigerian woman who was also a student, whom he eventually married.

After being disillusioned by the racism encountered while seeking a career in corporate America, he decided to seek alternatives. In 1977 he and his Chinwe moved to Nigeria where he took four-year appointment as a lecturer of Government at a Boy's High School in Benin City.

While in Nigeria he appeared on Nigeria Television on many occasions, wrote poetry and in his leisure time worked on his 1982 Novel, The Black Expatriate in Africa. In 1981 Larry and his wife Chinwe returned to the U.S. His wife subsequently developed health problems in 1984 and passed away in May 1985. Since then, he has mourned his wife, worked as a Community Services Executive in the OMI Community of San Francisco (twelve years) and an Elementary and Secondary Teacher.

Larry is a Professional Educator in the Bay Area. Ukali completed Journey *To The Motherland, from San Francisco To Benin City* and it was published in 2002. Between 2002 and 2004 Larry completed *History To Destiny Through Afrocentric Poetry* and a Master's of Education. Ukali also has a new book in the works called:

American Challenges In The Obama Era now available as a kindle e-book.

American Challenges In The Obama Era

By:
Larry Ukali Johnson-Redd

Here is the Amazon.com link:

http://www.amazon.com/s/ref=nb_sb_noss?url=searchalias%
3Dstripbooks&fieldkeywords=Journey+To+The+Motherland+
from+San+francisco+to+Benin+City#/ref=nb_sb_url=search-
alias%3Ddigital-text&fieldkeywords=American+Challenges+In+The+Oba
ma+Era+Part+1&rh=n%3A13

Postscript

Well now you have read Long Distance Love what do you think of my experiences good bad and ugly? Was she a 419 queen or was this a real love gone badly? Why? Why not?

After this relationship was well over I was still slightly blinded by love so I wrote this book in part to make sense of this whole scenario and occurrences of it all and found the story Long Distance Love!

And my Nigerian friends in Nigeria told me that my fiancé was a fake maybe I should have listened to them and washed my hands clean of her right there in Nigeria! Write me by going to the email button at ljredd52@aol.com or my facebook page

Let me know if this was a 419 scheme Queen or a real love gone badly!

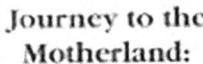

Journey to the Motherland:

From San Francisco to Benin City

Larry Ukali Johnson-Redd

Six Reasons To Read Journey To The Motherland From San Francisco to Benin City

*New price of Journey To The Motherland on Amazon.com $4.00 only plus shipping costs!

*New price on Loving Black Women (Audio Version only until Oct.1, 2010)

$5.00 only plus shipping costs. However Loving Black Women will also be released as a Kindle book very soon!

http://www.nathanielturner.com/larryuklaijohnsonreddtable.htm

*Link to Amazon.com is here: Go to this link and click on the image of the book or on the link to my page at the bottom of the table!

http://www.youtube.com/user/ukalitheafrican

1. Read Journey to understand how Africans particularly Nigerians viewed a brother in their midst from San Francisco, CA USA in the late 70's!

2. Buy this book to understand our ties to our African motherland and the cultural experiences of an urban African-American in Nigeria for a 4-year stay.!

3. Learn how the author's experiences will change your views on Africa! This book has a sequel type connection to Long Distance Love and is based on my experiences while living in Nigeria from 1977 to 1981..

4. Buy this book and be transported to Africa while reading this book!

5. Buy this book to understand Africa better in the historical and contemporary basis!

6. Read this book that tells a positive Black story about a San Francisco born Black Man who graduates from 2 universities and travels to Nigeria, West Africa, our homeland for Africans all over the world. Once you read Journey To The Motherland give it to the Nigerian, Nigerian-American, African-American or West Indian-Caribbean you feel needs to read this book the most! A review of Journey To The Motherland by an African-American sister.

BOOK REVIEW by Veronica Brown Printed in the African Times Newspaper based in Los Angeles, California 03/17/03: Journey To The Motherland, From San Francisco To Benin City—Nigeria, written by Larry Ukali Johnson-Redd

If you are looking for some enlightenment, read this book Journey To The Motherland, From San Francisco To Benin City by Larry Ukali Johnson-Redd. It is a revelation of one man's insight and involvement in the political arena of racism towards Black students in this country especially in the 60's and sadly to say still continues in today's society not only in the South but also in the West. The struggles, hardships they had to endure in order to obtain a decent education to better their lives in comparison to their white counterparts.

The first chapter opens with him and his wife returning from the motherland and in one solitude moment on the plane his thoughts flashes back to his youth in the city of San Francisco where he was born.

The next three or four chapters tell you of his days in junior and senior high school. His problems at securing a job was not with (out) its complications, event though his credentials were impressive and impressive they were however he persevered and conquered.

When both he and his wife accepted new posts in Africa, he as a teacher and she to work for the government, it was the most important decision any two people in love with each other could have made. For his wife, it was the best thing that could have happened because she was returning to her country of her birth and he was going there for the first time to his *Homeland*. The description of places and the cities he visited and most of all the people of Africa were awe-inspiring *one only had to close their eyes and you can feel, hear and smell all the beauty and the sufferings that made Africa the great Continent she is and then you are suddenly transported there.*

His description of family greetings, the meeting of old friends and the making of new friends and the making of new ones was something to treasure for a lifetime. While living in Africa he gives one the feeling that you never want leave once you get there, it was like coming home to heaven on earth, His time spent there was the most remarkable of his life with his wife along his side could not have completed a better picture. Much as he loved Africa, he still longed to be back home in America where his family still lived. He returned only to lose his wife and settled back to life in America.

Journey to the Motherland: From San Francisco to Benin City

After being disillusioned by racism in corporate America, San Francisco born *Larry Ukali Johnson-Redd* and his Nigerian wife move to Benin City in Nigeria to seek new alternatives, whereupon he accepts a four-year appointment as a lecturer of government at a boys' high school.

In Nigeria the couple discover and re-discover personal and social challenges that are skillfully presented in a dream sequence that begins in the U.S. with the author as a student activist in 1967, and ends in the 1980's when he and his wife return to the United States.

The luminous autobiographical manifesto represents a continuing and progressive sociological exposé on the intersection and fluidity of cross-cultural understanding.

Journey to the Motherland is honestly rendered, making all the sentiments palpably real and strikingly descriptive of the people and idiosyncrasies of Nigeria. Ukali has made a beautiful effort to give flavor to where he has been, where he is coming from, and where he intends to go.

Adeyinka Fashokun, Ed.D.
Visiting Professor, Stanford Language Center, Stanford University;
Principal, Brenkwitz High School, Hayward, California

This work is a fantastic rite of passage story that places African social consciousness at the forefront of personal challenge, with dashing doses of reality. Readers will find *Journey to the Motherland: From San Francisco to Benin City* entertaining and culturally intriguing.

Itibari M. Zulu, Th.D.
Ralph J. Bunche Center for African American Studies at UCLA;
Provost, Amen-Ra Theological Seminary, Los Angeles

ISBN 0-9674226-3-9 $14.95

 Amen-Ra Theological Seminary Press
10920 Wilshire Boulevard, Suite 150-9132
Los Angeles, CA 90024-6502

"Journey To The Motherland – From San Francisco to Benin City"
Novel by Larry Ukali Johnson-Redd

Review By Kola Thomas

San Francisco, CA

This autobiographical "Journey To The Motherland" is a 160-page novel, but I read it in less than two days. Reading this book was an invocation of the nostalgia to be "at home right now."

This book is written in a style that helps the reader to be transported to Africa and be actively engaged in the dynamic and evolving events of the moment as they unfold. One could not help but follow the "Journey..." and soak in the moments. Perhaps being a Yoruba (born in Nigeria), familiar with the local terrain and socio-cultural manifestations and political landscape of Nigeria; and living in the Bay Area for over twenty-five years—well I travel home periodically—I am able to understand the book better. However, this is a book about a wonderful experience in Africa.

One thing that is clear throughout the book is a commitment by the author Ukali Johnson-Redd, to increasing empowerment for African people all over the world.

It behooves any one contemplating a visit to any part of Africa; to read "Journey..." A great many brothers and sisters go to Africa, without preparation or some form of orientation. They then experience cultural shock on arrival—shock at the mass of black people taking care of business; shock at the unparalleled and unqualified show of hospitality displayed by the hosts; shock at the high level of intellectual capacity and scholarship; shock at the fact that people are unfazed at whether or not utilities work; and shock at the fact that the urban and rural areas are just as any you will find in the so-called civilized western cities.

I could not help but be thankfully amazed at how Brother Ukali has assimilated the local lingo and nuances to a "T." Talk about "*invigilation…*" for proctoring a student test - page 124; and dispensing "*dongoyaro*" – a traditional herbal extract - as the preferred medication for malaria - page 144 - that follows age-long African understanding of traditional therapy – and which Western medicine refuses to celebrate. Perhaps Ukali needs to consider sharing his experience at medical colleges here in the United States.

"Journey to Motherland…" is recommended and a definite must read by every one who wishes to get a better understanding of Africa and African ways, its indubitable and welcoming hospitality, and its great culture, educational environment.

Kola Akintola-Thomas is CEO of African Global Institute-USA based in San Francisco, California. He can be reached at africanglobal@yahoo.com

Amazon.com link for Journey To The motherland from San Francisco To Benin City

http://www.amazon.com/Journey-Motherland-Francisco-Benin-City/dp/0967422639/ref=sr_1_1?
s=books&ie=UTF8&qid=1366060925&sr=1-
1&keywords=Journey+To+The+Motherland+from+San+francisco
+to+Benin+City

If you missed this event the San Francisco Kings of Poetry Saturday April 10, 2010 or attended and enjoyed it do not worry a DVD will soon be available for purchase on my page at Amazon.com and/ or available on You Tube! Here are the Poets who participated in the Kings of Poetry from right to left, Larry Ukali Johnson-Redd, Paradise, Terry Moore and Larry Ware.

Busy Lagos, Nigeria

Busy Lagos again

http://www.amazon.com/Journey-Motherland-
Francisco-Benin-City/dp/0967422639/ref=sr_1_1?
s=books&ie=UTF8&qid=1366060925&sr=1-
1&keywords=Journey+To+The+Motherland+from+San+francisco
+to+Benin+City

Reviews by 5 Strong Black Women Of Loving Black Women By Larry Ukali Johnson-Redd Books by Larry Ukali Johnson-Redd/ Journey to the Motherland on sale for $4.oo at Amazon.com / History To Destiny Through Afrocentric Poetry / Loving Black Women on sale for $5.00 on Amazon.com! History to Destiny Through Afrocentric Poetry is out of print! New Books-Long Distance Love a Memoir about my engagement to a Nigerian Sister and my 2005 trip to Nigeria! I am looking for a new literary agent to present this potential best seller to Publishers! And my newest manuscript titled, Black Lines: Black Rhymes, African-American Challenges in the Obama Era! Subtitle Why African-Americans Should Love Each Other, Africa and Africans All Over The World! By: Larry Ukali Johnson-Redd—you guessed it, I need a literary agent who will present this book to Publishers too! Read the reviews and after reading the reviews go to Loving Black Women Part 1 at YouTube.com and check out all 9 clips. Here are 5 Reviews of my book Loving Black Women by 5 strong Black Women! They are Martha Kimbrough, Mukulla Godwin, Pearl Jr., author of Black Women Need Love Too! Cheryl Robinson. Www. JustAboutBooksTalkShow.com and Linda Mayfield-Hayes author of Afroetry; Afrocentric Poetry that Educates!

* * * * *

Loving Black Women

WAF RATING: ☆☆☆☆

Larry Ukali Johnson-Redd, Author/Poet
Amen-Ra Theological Seminary Press
Release Date: May 2006
Paperback/2 Audio2CD Set—List Price: $5.00
ISBN: 0-9674226-6-3

*Now available as one of my 4 e-books for only
$ .99 at my Amazon.com/Kindle page*

Loving Black Women starts as an essay and the book ends with poetry. The author starts the essay with two basic themes: improving the way African Americans see each other and to have nurturing realistic and wholesome relationships as brothers and sisters. Johnson-Redd goes on to say that this must be done despite racial discrimination, political domination and white supremacy.

Along with preserving the relationship between brothers and sisters, the essay transitions into a global discussion. Here the author begins to suggest that Africans are spread throughout the United States, Caribbean, Central and South America, Saudi Arabia, Pakistan, India and other areas of the Middle East and Asia. Since Africans have a dominant presence around the globe, there should be a dialogue to battle racism, oppression and genocide.

The majority of the essay is a discussion about Black on Black killing. He makes a contrast between the violence that is taking place in the Sudan and what happens in the community where he is from, San Francisco. He suggests that people don't understand the continent of Africa and seldom see Africans conducting modern business in a modern environment. The essay is a great historical and informative overview of what African Americans face in the United States and what Africans endure on the continent of Africa.

After the essay, Johnson-Redd delights the readers with poetry. He has an unquenchable love for the African woman and sees her as the most beautiful creature on earth. He also has wonderful pictures to go along with the poetry. This book is clearly written for those who delight themselves in the beautiful African woman, and it enlightens one on political issues that Africans across the glove have in common.

Martha Kimbrough
WAF Book Reviewer

ORDER NOW

* * * * * 2 I Like It (4 Stars): All Ways/Always Loving a Sister! Loving Black Women is a book of poetry offering ideas to improve the many complicated ways that brothers and sisters love each other. It is also a common sense approach to black politics and white supremacy overcoming racial discrimination and political domination. This is a thought-provoking read that enlightens and educates us as a people. Larry is a man who loves his heritage and loves black women! Cheryl Robinson.
Www.JustAboutBooksTalkShow.com

- * * * 3 Larry Ukali Johnson Redd's book, Loving Black Women left me pleasantly surprised. I was expecting a book of love poems dedicated to black women, but this book is so much more. This compilation of poems also shows a deep love towards motherland Africa and our proud African heritage. I particularly liked: Tribute to All African

- Women, The Beauty of a Sister, I Know You Know Why, and my favorite: Tree of Life part 1 You are The tree of life You are The source of spice You are The carrier of our black seed You are All we really need You are The source of our civilization You are The mother of our Black Nation The world is rough And full of strife But you, you are Our precious tree of life In a time when black women are thought of and categorized in less favorable terms, this book, "Loving Black Women" is a refreshing, and much needed change.

- Linda Mayfield-Hayes author of Afroetry; Afrocentric Poetry that Educates & Motivates.

- * * * * 4 TRUBUTE TO A TRIBUTE Praises are due to Larry Ukali Johnson-Redd's newest literary accomplishment, Loving Black Women." For as an African woman, I am proud of this brother's ability to give explanations as to what removal of black love has inevitably led to, that being self-hate which in turn creates loathing, rejection and violence towards those most like the self. Mr. Johnson-Redd's book should be a must read for those who ask the question, "Why is there so much violence in the Black community?" Mr. Johnson is a true teacher, and instructor of Black life, Black Love. He answers the questions of the causes of self-destructive violence very well when he states in several of his poems/spoken word selections that there is such a pressing need to reclaim love for each other, to heal, to acknowledge our identity as an African people and for the Black man to pay tribute to the Black woman so that unity of mind, spirit and purpose can be achieved, our very survival depends on this. Mr. Johnson-Redd highlights many positive things in his very flowing, easy to read style, which facilitates the comprehension of several essential concepts. These include the need for the African psyche to become whole, that is to eliminate the fragmentation between the male/female psyches caused by the malevolent influence of White Supremacy. He states that: "this white American racism is the most dangerous force of evil in the world." Yet Mr. Johnson-Redd does not dwell on this premise. Instead, he formulates insights for survival. He yearns for unity within the African Diaspora, and equates love as the foundation for renewing the Black self, family, and nation. His suggestion that there be an 8th and 9th All African People's Congress should be heeded. As an African woman, I can only thank Mr. Johnson-Redd for his respect for and praises to the Black woman. In his expressions of consciousness and gratitude are found hope that we are indeed a people "who can overcome all obstacles.

Mukulla Godwin * * * * *

"5 Loving Black Women One night last week, I was having a very tough time falling asleep so I decided to do some reading and the first book on my list was, "Loving Black Women" by Larry Ukali Johnson Redd. I was expecting to read lots of loving poetry, but the book was a lot more. The way the author wrote about the need to collaborate all the African peoples together to develop a movement of Black self-love was so much more than conscious awakening, it was profound enough to allow my fantasies to travel to Africa and be a part of a worldwide solution against White Supremacy that promotes Black unity, which is tied to the end of racism as a form to oppress Black people worldwide. Author, Larry Ukali Johnson Redd is highly educated due to obtaining his formal university degrees, but his intellect went beyond just skimming the surface because he was able to articulate a seemingly complex problem into a few short pages that encourage movement toward solidarity and racial harmony. The poems in this book were so contagious that I read each one of them and when I finished with his emotional and in-touch mastery of the English language, I was able to finally fall asleep, but this time with a smile on my face knowing that someone really loves and values Black women completely, and come to realize that Mr. Johnson-Redd is an important voice for Black worldwide unity. Pearl Jr., author of Black Women Need Love Too!

http://www.blackwomenneedlovet oo.com/

- *********Larry Ukali Johnson-Redd*********
- http://www.conversationsofafri ca.asmnetwork.net/

By Larry Ukali Johnson-Redd, author of Loving Black Women

Please check out History To Destiny Through Afrocentric Poetry available as a Kindle E-book for only $.99 cents and it will on your media in 60 seconds anywhere in the world.

Publication Date: **January 7, 2012**

My reading of Mr. Larry Ukali Johnson-Redd's, " History to Destiny Through Afrocentric Poetry", was full of poems that radiated with the spirit, the voices and the cry of the elders and our ancestors.

To me, this poetry expresses the great need for the Africans in America to unite with each other and unite with Africans in the Diaspora as well as with Africans all over the world -as a conscious priority.

Comments written by the late Nashid Hakim Ahmad R.I.P. Nashid was my good friend during his life. LUJR

www.ingramcontent.com/pod-product-compliance
Lightning Source LLC
Chambersburg PA
CBHW051139120626
46547CB00012B/873